Word 6 for Windows
explained

ALSO AVAILABLE

Word 6 for Windows explained

by

N. Kantaris
and
P.R.M. Oliver

**BERNARD BABANI (publishing) LTD
THE GRAMPIANS
SHEPHERDS BUSH ROAD
LONDON W6 7NF
ENGLAND**

PLEASE NOTE

Although every care has been taken with the production of this book to ensure that any projects, designs, modifications and/or programs, etc., contained herewith, operate in a correct and safe manner and also that any components specified are normally available in Great Britain, the Publishers and Author(s) do not accept responsibility in any way for the failure (including fault in design) of any project, design, modification or program to work correctly or to cause damage to any equipment that it may be connected to or used in conjunction with, or in respect of any other damage or injury that may be so caused, nor do the Publishers accept responsibility in any way for the failure to obtain specified components.

Notice is also given that if equipment that is still under warranty is modified in any way or used or connected with home-built equipment then that warranty may be void.

First Published – October 1994
Reprinted – September 1995

British Library Cataloguing in Publication Data:

Kantaris, Noel
  Word 6 for Windows Explained
  I. Title II. Oliver, Phil
  652.55369

ISBN 0 85934 354 5

Cover design by Gregor Arthur
Cover illustration by Adam Willis
Printed and Bound in Great Britain by Cox & Wyman Ltd, Reading

ABOUT THIS BOOK

Word 6 for Windows Explained has been written for those who want to get to grips with the Microsoft Word for Windows (version 6) word processor and desk top publishing package in the fastest possible time. No previous knowledge is assumed, but the book does not describe how to set up your computer hardware, or how to install Microsoft Windows. If you need to know more about these topics, then may we suggest that you also refer to the book *A Concise User's Guide to Windows 3.1* (BP325), and to either *A Concise User's Guide to MS-DOS 5* (BP318), or *MS-DOS 6 Explained* (BP341), depending on the version of your Disc Operating System. These books are also published by BERNARD BABANI (publishing) Ltd.

This book was written with the busy person in mind. It is not necessary to read several hundred pages covering all there is to know about a subject, when a few selected pages can do the same thing quite adequately! With the help of this book, it is hoped that you will be able to get the most out of Word for Windows and your computer in terms of efficiency, productivity and enjoyment, and that you will be able to do it in the shortest, most effective and informative way.

More emphasis has been placed on an understanding of what we consider to be the critical areas in the program, such as page layout, paragraph styles and the use of frames, than on a general overall description of the package, although we have tried to make the book as complete as possible.

The Word for Windows package is the leading Windows word processor and, we feel, will stand comparison with anything else available today in the marketplace.

ABOUT THE AUTHORS

Noel Kantaris graduated in Electrical Engineering at Bristol University and after spending three years in the Electronics Industry in London, took up a Tutorship in Physics at the University of Queensland. Research interests in Ionospheric Physics, led to the degrees of M.E. in Electronics and Ph.D. in Physics. On return to the UK, he took up a Post-Doctoral Research Fellowship in Radio Physics at the University of Leicester, and then in 1973 a lecturing position in Engineering at the Camborne School of Mines, Cornwall, (part of Exeter University), where since 1978 he has also assumed the responsibility for the Computing Department.

Phil Oliver graduated in Mining Engineering at Camborne School of Mines in 1967 and since then has specialised in most aspects of surface mining technology, with a particular emphasis on computer related techniques. He has worked in Guyana, Canada, several Middle Eastern countries, South Africa and the United Kingdom, on such diverse projects as: the planning and management of bauxite, iron, gold and coal mines; rock excavation contracting in the UK; international mining equipment sales and technical back up and international mine consulting for a major mining house in South Africa. In 1988 he took up a lecturing position at Camborne School of Mines (part of Exeter University) in Surface Mining and Management.

ACKNOWLEDGEMENTS

We would like to thank the staff of Microsoft UK for the provision of software for the preparation of this book. We would also like to thank colleagues at the Camborne School of Mines for the helpful tips and suggestions which assisted us in the writing of this book.

TRADEMARKS

CONTENTS

1. PACKAGE OVERVIEW

Microsoft's Word for Windows is the best selling Windows word processor and is fully integrated with Microsoft Office and the Microsoft Windows environment. In all the Windows versions Word has had a leaning towards desk top publishing which offers fully editable WYSIWYG (what you see is what you get) modes that can be viewed in various zoom levels, including full page. Couple this with the ability to include and manipulate full colour graphics and you can see the enormous power of the program. Once you have overcome the first hurdle and started to use Word 6 for Windows, you will find it both intuitive and an easy program to produce the type of word processed output you would not have dreamt possible.

Hardware Requirements

To install Word 6 for Windows, you need an IBM AT compatible or PS/2 computer equipped with an Intel 80286 or higher processor, an EGA or higher resolution video adapter, a 3½" high-density floppy disc drive, and 4 MB or more RAM. You also require both MS-DOS 3.1 or later, and Windows 3.1 or later. However, to get the best out of the package, you will need as a minimum system configuration an 80386 processor and VGA resolution screen.

The SETUP program allows you to select one of three installations: 'Typical' which installs the files you need to use the most common features of Word, as well as Word Art and Graph (requires at least 15 MB of hard disc space), 'Complete/Custom' which installs the whole Word package or selected components (the complete package requires at least 24 MB of hard disc space), or 'Laptop' which is the minimum installation and requires about 6 MB of hard disc space.

Although it is possible to operate from the keyboard alone, the availability of a mouse is a must if you are going to benefit from the program's features and from Window's Graphical User Interface (GUI). After all, pointing and clicking at an option on the screen, is a lot easier than having to learn several different key combinations. So, if you can, install a mouse.

Major Word Features

Some of the major features Word for Windows 6 contains, include the ability to:

- Drag and drop when editing text and tables in a document - this is more convenient than cutting and pasting.

- Create documents that have different formatting, multiple columns, and a variety of page layouts.

- Create styles that include a combination of formats, such as indented paragraphs, bold text, or borders.

- Replace the formatting in an entire document, and a style in parts of a document with another style.

- Add comments and annotations to a document without changing the original text.

- Use revision marks so that intended changes can be seen easily - such changes can then be accepted or rejected.

- Create a glossary of text and graphics which can be inserted in any part of a document.

- Insert footnotes in any part of a document's page with automatic numbering.

- Remove selectively from the display screen the toolbar, the ruler, the scroll bars, and the status bar, so as to provide a larger working area which might appeal to some users.

- Correct your spelling with an extensive spell checker - you can even add special words to it.

- Check a document's grammar and style and customise the latter to suit your needs.

- Look up the meaning of words and find synonyms with the use of the thesaurus.

- Create tables in a document, which can contain text, numbers, pictures and objects - formatting can be applied to the whole, or individual parts of it.

- Add pictures created in another application to a document, scale them proportionally, or crop them to requirement.

- Ability to create objects, such as graphs, charts and equations, which can be modified, edited, moved and/or copied.

- Insert a frame around a paragraph, picture or object, then move the frame and its contents, or change its size.

- View documents in a variety of ways, preview a document before printing, print a document or print/view information about a document.

- Automated printing of envelopes, provided the printer's envelope feeder has been installed.

- Organise documents by using outlines to structure text, modify such outlines, and create a table of contents.

- Use a find-file facility to search documents for a specified subject, ability to browse the text and graphics within such document files before opening them, and view information about them.

- Use on-line tutorials to help you with Word for Windows, and a much enhanced context sensitive Help command.

- Use the optional user's help to ease the change from WordPerfect to Word for Windows.

- Transparently import existing files produced by most versions of Microsoft and WordPerfect word processors, as well as worksheets and databases produced in Excel, Lotus 1-2-3, and dBase formats.

- Link and embed information or objects (OLE) created in other Windows applications into a Word document.

- Network the program so users can share information.

New Features in Word 6:

Word for Windows 6 has many new features over and above those found in previous versions of the program. These include:

- Drag and drop text and graphics across windows.

- Shortcut menus relevant to the type of work you are carrying out at the time, to help speed your work.

- Letter Wizard which, with the help of pre-written business letters, gives you a big head start in creating your own style business letters.

- AutoCorrect which fixes common typing errors as you work.

- AutoText which speeds up the addition of frequently used text, tables, lists, and graphics, into your document. This was known as 'Glossary' in previous versions of Word.

- AutoFormat which analyses a document and suggests a formatting style. By accepting the suggestion you can quickly format all or part of a document.

- Table Wizard which helps you quickly create and format a table.

- Bullets and Numbering command which can easily add bullets and numbers to multiple-level lists.

- Heading Numbering command which can create numbered headings with built-in heading styles.

- AutoCaption which helps you to quickly add captions and create cross-references to captions, headings, tables, and other items.

- Full screen view ability to maximise the text area on your screen by hiding menus, toolbars, rulers, etc.

In addition, Word 6 has several new editing and formatting options, as well as a new mail merge tool. It also has an easier to use interface with toolbars providing more buttons where you need them.

Icons and Toolbar

Word for Windows supports numerous buttons which are to be found in the Toolbar, underneath the menu bar, at the top of the screen. These are colourful icons, or buttons, that give you mouse click access to the functions most often used in the program. You can use the ToolTips to find out about toolbar buttons.

The usual drop menus are still present but need only be used if a button does not exist to perform the required function.

To obtain a description of what an icon button can do when clicked, point to it and pause for a few seconds. This causes a description of the icon function to appear immediately below it. To select a given function point to the appropriate icon and click the left mouse button.

A further selection of buttons are placed on the Ribbon, to be found immediately below the Toolbar, as shown below:

These buttons allow you to format and enhance your text in various ways. The Ribbon contains a font box which shows the font currently being used, and gives access to the rest of the installed fonts. Another button lets you change the font size, while others allow you to change the attributes of the font, such as italic and underline. Further buttons allow you to change justification of pre-selected text, or set different types of tabs.

Styles and Templates:

Word differs in one basic way from most DOS based word processors in that it uses styles to control the formatting of paragraphs and pages within a document, and templates to create a wide variety of different types of documents, such as memos, letters, reports, academic articles, and legal briefs. Templates are files that can contain text, graphics, formatting instructions, macros, and styles.

Once you get accustomed to using styles and templates, you will find they save you an enormous amount of time with document formatting. Once a style is changed, the changes are reflected everywhere the style is used. You can even create a 'next' style to always follow a given style. Word for Windows comes with nearly 30 pre-defined templates. With these alone you should be able to create attractive and functional letters, memos, reports, books, etc., but you can also modify these in any way you like to make completely new templates for your documents.

Installing Word for Windows

Installing Word on your computer's hard disc is made very easy with the use of the SETUP program on Disc 1. You need to run this program because part of its job is to convert compressed files from the distribution discs prior to copying them onto your hard disc; it then configures Windows to run Word.

Insert the Microsoft Word for Windows distribution disc #1 into drive A: and start the installation from the Program Manager of Windows, by clicking your mouse on **File**, followed by **Run** and typing

        A:setup

in the dialogue box, as shown below:

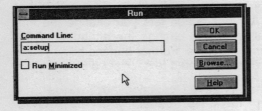

The first time you do this you will be asked to type your name on the initial screen produced. Word will generate a set of initials for you which may be used later, if you carry out document correction, for example.

Word then initialises SETUP ready for the transfer of files and displays a screen offering you the default drive and directory on which it proposes to transfer the program files as

        C:WINWORD

You could change the default drive if you do not have the required space on drive C: (we have selected drive D:), and also the directory (a better name might be WINWORD6). SETUP creates the specified directory on the preferred drive, and searches your system for installed components. It then displays the screen shown below:

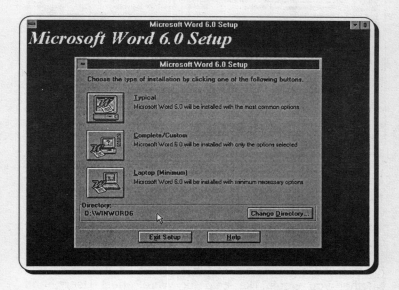

If you choose to install the 'Complete/Custom' option which requires 24 MB of disc space, do note that even though you might select a drive other than the C: drive for the installation of Word, SETUP installs seven common applications in a subdirectory called MSAPPS under your WINDOWS directory. These common applications require at least 6 MB of hard disc space on the drive that holds your Windows package. The rest of the program will be installed on to your selected drive.

Thus, selecting the 'Complete/Custom' installation displays the screen shown on the next page.

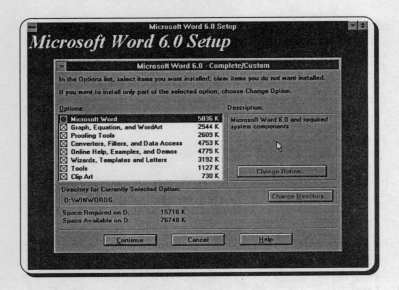

This is the main installation menu which will be repeated if you re-activate SETUP and select to change your installation. It is from here that you can add or subtract various components of the program.

Selecting the **Continue** button causes SETUP to search for installed components of the program. It then asks you whether you would like help for WordPerfect Users, and finally, if you have enough hard disc space for the chosen installation, asks you to which Group of Applications you would like the package to be added - we suggest you accept the default option which is 'Microsoft Office'.

If all is well, SETUP starts to unpack its files to the specified hard disc and directory. While this takes place, some information appears on the screen, namely about the new features in Word 6, as shown on the next page. This goes on until another distribution disc is required to be inserted in the A: drive.

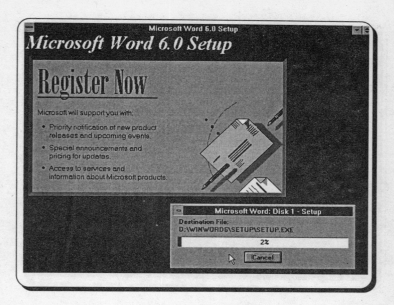

If the complete package is installed, 11 high density distribution discs will be used, and will take well over an hour. The % bar indicates the number of files transferred rather than a percentage of total time required, so the first four discs take much longer than the rest.

If the installation is successful, SETUP inserts the following icons to the Microsoft Office Icon Group of the Windows Program Manager:

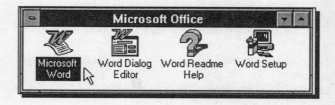

Finally, SETUP displays its final 'Restart Windows' screen, shown on the next page.

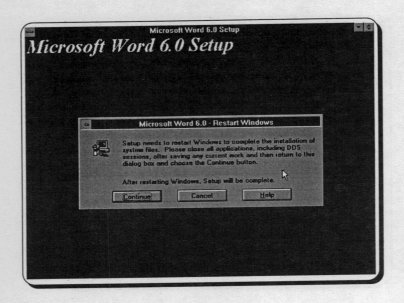

If you are running any other Windows applications while installing Word, you will have to close them down as SETUP needs to restart Windows, after which the program is ready to be activated and used.

2. THE WORD ENVIRONMENT

Starting the Program

To start Word, as long as the WINWORD directory is included on your system path, you need only type the words **win winword** at the C:\> prompt. Otherwise you must specify the complete path to the directory in the command as follows:

   win D:\WINWORD\winword

if D: is the drive on which the program was installed.

It is more usual however to start the program when Windows is already running as explained below.

Word Program Icons:

The install program opens a new group window in the Program Manager of Windows and names it **Microsoft Office** as shown below. Four icons are placed in this window.

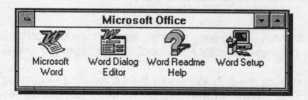

These icons are self-explanatory; the first starts Word, the second is an advanced feature used in the creation of dialogue boxes for use with Word macros, while the third could contain late information on several topics and, if so, could either be read on the screen or printed on paper. The fourth icon activates the SETUP program which searches your hard disc for components of the program, then displays the screen shown on the next page.

You can leave this group window intact, or move the icons to one of your other Application Windows (by dragging them between the two windows with the left mouse button depressed) and then delete the Group window with the **File** and **Delete** commands while it is selected. Manipulating icons or windows will be described more fully in the next chapter which deals with the Windows environment.

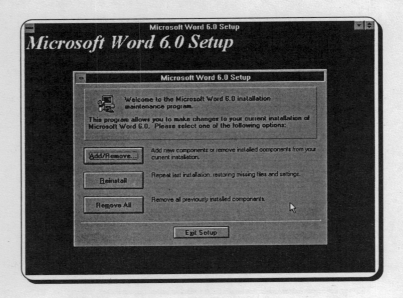

From this set-up screen, you can add or remove components of the package, reinstall the package, or remove the whole package.

Word is started in Windows by either double-clicking the left mouse button on the 'Microsoft Word' icon, or by double clicking on a Word document file (with the extension .doc) in the Windows File Manager. In the latter case the document will be loaded into Word at the same time.

To start Word with the keyboard from within Windows, open the Windows Program Manager, then use the <Ctrl+Tab> key combination (while holding the <Ctrl> key down, press the <Tab> key), until the Microsoft Office Group is highlighted, then use the cursor keys to highlight the Microsoft Word application icon, and press the <Enter> key.

The first time you start Word from within the Windows Program Manager, causes the display of the 'Tip of the Day'. You could easily spend a lot of time reading the numerous useful tips by clicking at the **Next Tip** button. If you would like a different tip to appear every time you start Word, then place the mouse pointer on the little square at the bottom of the window and click the left mouse button to check it.

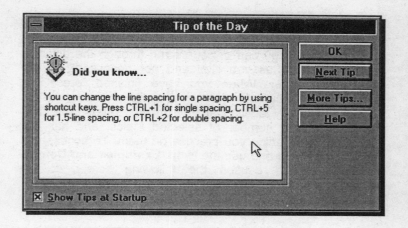

Getting Familiar with Word

Word has two options under the **Help** menu which allow you to familiarise yourself with the package; **Quick Preview** and **Examples and Demos**.

The first one of these, is a show tutorial. To access it, use the **Help, Quick Preview** command which displays:

This tutorial is a good introduction to the powerful features of Word. It takes about half an hour to work through and is well worth the time. You can of course run through the different options as often as you like, and not necessarily in the presentation order. When you have finished, press the **Return to Word** button.

The second familiarisation option offers detailed information on a number of selected topics, and has the added ability of letting you practice on them. To access this option, start Word and use the **Help, Examples and Demos** command, which causes the following screen to be displayed.

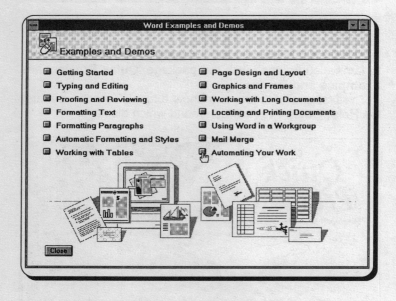

As you can see from the list above, this option gives you far more detailed information on a much larger selection of topics. We suggest you return to this option often to build up your knowledge of the package.

The Word Screen

The opening 'blank' screen of Word for Windows is shown below. It is perhaps worth spending some time looking at the various parts that make up this screen, or window. Word follows the usual Microsoft Windows conventions and if you are familiar with these you can skip through this section. Otherwise a few minutes might be well spent here.

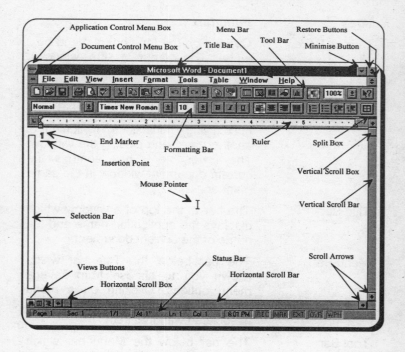

The window as shown takes up the full screen area available. If you click on the application restore button, the top one of the two restore buttons at the top right of the screen, you can make Word show in a smaller window. This can be useful when you are running several applications at the same time and you want to transfer between them with the mouse.

Note that the Word window, which in this case displays an empty document with the title 'Document1', has a solid 'Title bar', indicating that it is the active application window.

Although multiple windows can be displayed simultaneously, you can only enter data into the active window (which will always be displayed on top). Title bars of non active windows appear a lighter shade than that of the active one.

The Word screen is divided into several areas which have the following functions. These are described from the top of the screen down, working from left to right.

Area	Function
Control Boxes	Clicking on the top control menu box, (upper left corner of the window), displays the pull-down Control menu which can be used to control the program window. It includes commands for re-sizing, moving, maximising, minimising, switching to another task, and closing the window. The lower menu box controls the current document window in the same manner.
Title Bar	The bar at the top of a window which displays the application name and the name of the current document.
Menu Bar	The bar below the Title bar which allows you to choose from several menu options. Clicking on a menu item displays the pull-down menu associated with that item.
Tool Bar	The bar below the Menu bar which contains buttons that give you mouse click access to the functions most often used in the program. These are grouped according to function, for example, the first three buttons deal with file manipulation, the next four with editing functions, etc.

Restore Buttons	When clicked on, these buttons restore the active window to the position and size occupied before being maximised or minimised. The restore button is then replaced by a Maximise button, with a single up-pointing arrow, which can be used to set the window to its former size.
Minimise Box	The button you point to and click to store an application as an icon (small symbol) at the bottom of the screen. Double clicking on such an icon will restore the screen and even maintain the cursor position.
Formatting Bar	The buttons on the Formatting Bar allow you to change the attributes of a font, such as italic and underline, and also to format text in various ways. The Formatting Bar contains three boxes; a style box, a font box and a size box which show which style, font and size of characters are currently being used. These boxes give access to other installed styles, fonts and character sizes.
Ruler	The area where you can see and set tabulation points and indents.
Split Box	The area to the extreme right of the Ruler which when dragged allows you to split the screen.
Scroll Bars	The areas on the screen (extreme right and bottom of each window) that contain scroll boxes in vertical and horizontal bars. Clicking on these bars allows you to control the part of a document which is visible on the screen.

Scroll Arrows	The arrowheads at each end of each scroll bar at which you can click to scroll the screen up and down one line, or left and right 10% of the screen, at a time.
Selection Bar	The area on the screen in the left margin of the Word window (marked here with a box for convenience), where the mouse pointer changes to an arrow that slants to the right. Clicking the left mouse once selects the current line, while clicking twice selects the current paragraph.
Views Buttons	Clicking these alternate views buttons changes views quickly.
Status Bar	The bottom line of the screen that displays information relating to your document, and in which a short description appears on what a button does when you point and click at it.

The Menu Bar Options:

Each menu bar option has associated with it a pull-down sub-menu. To activate the menu, either press the <Alt> key, which causes the first option of the menu (in this case the Document Control Menu box) to be highlighted, then use the right and left arrow keys to highlight any of the options in the menu, or use the mouse to point to an option. Pressing either the <Enter> key, or the left mouse button, reveals the pull-down sub-menu of the highlighted menu option. The sub-menu of the **File** option is shown on the next page.

Menu options can also be activated directly by pressing the <Alt> key followed by the underlined letter of the required option. Thus, pressing <Alt+F>, causes the pull-down **File** sub-menu to be displayed. You can use the up and down arrow keys to move the highlighted bar up and down a sub-menu, or the right and left arrow keys to move along the options in the menu bar. Note that as you move up and down a sub-menu the status bar shows a brief description of the highlighted option. Pressing the <Enter> key selects the highlighted option or executes the highlighted command. Pressing the <Esc> key once, closes the pull-down sub-menu, while pressing the <Esc> key for a second time, closes the menu system.

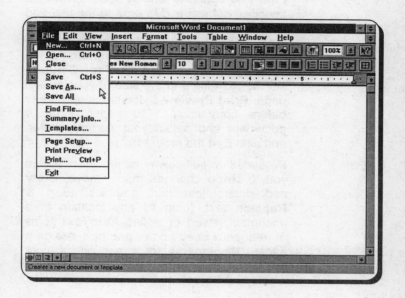

Some of the sub-menu options can be accessed with 'quick key' combinations from the keyboard. Such combinations are shown on the drop-down menus, for example, <Ctrl+S> is the quick key for the **Save** option in the **File** sub-menu. If a sub-menu option is not available, at any time, it will display in a grey colour. Some menu options only appear in Word when that tool is being used, but the ones described on the next page remain constant.

The following is a brief description of the standard menu options. For a more detailed description of each sub-menu item, either highlight it and read the text on the status bar, or use the on-line **Help** system, described later.

File

Produces a pull-down menu of mainly file related tasks, such as creating a **New** document, the ability to **Open**, or **Close** files, and **Save** files with the same name, or **Save As** a different name. You can use the **Find File** option to search documents for a specified subject and to browse the text and graphics within documents before opening them, view **Summary Information** about them, and change the **Template** or its options. Finally, you can use **Page Setup** to set the margins and the size of your printed page, **Print Preview** a document on screen before committing it to paper, **Print** a document and select your current printer, and also **Exit** the program.

Edit

Produces a pull-down menu which allows you to **Undo** changes made, move, **Copy** and delete text and graphics, **Find & Replace** text, jump to any location in a document, insert or define **AutoText** items of frequently used text or graphics, assign a name (**Bookmark**) to a section of your document, view and update **Links**, or open a selected **Object**.

View

Produces a pull-down menu which contains screen display options which allow you to change the editing view to **Normal** or **Outline**, display the page in **Page Layout** (WYSIWYG - what you see is what you get), or switch to **Master Document** mode (a document that takes some or all of its contents from one or more Word documents), control whether a **Full Screen** is displayed and whether the **Toolbars**, or **Ruler** are displayed, show a list of **Headers/Footers**, open windows for viewing **Footnotes**, or **Annotations**, and determine the scale of the editing view by using the **Zoom** option.

Insert   Produces a pull-down menu which allows you to insert **Breaks** to ends of pages, columns, or sections, add **Page Numbers** to a document, insert a comment and activate the **Annotation** pane. You can also insert the **Date and Time** into a document, a **Field** (instruction) for computed contents, special characters with **Symbol**, or a new **Form Field**, at the cursor position. In addition you can insert a **Footnote** reference, place a **Caption** above or below a selected object, or a **Cross-reference**. The **Index and Tables** option allows you to build an index entry, an index, or tables of contents, tables, etc. Finally, you can insert the contents of a **File**, an empty **Frame** (or frame selected text), a **Picture**, or an **Object** into the active document.

Format   Produces a pull-down menu which allows you to alter the appearance of text, both on the screen and when printed. Such features as font, size, colour, alignment, print spacing, justification, and enhancements (bold, underlined and italic) are included. You can change the appearance and line numbering of a selected **Paragraph**, set and clear **Tabs**, or change the **Border and Shading** of a selected paragraph, table cell(s), or picture. You can also change the **Columns** format of the selected section, **Change Case**, format the first character of a paragraph as a **Drop Cap**(ital), create bullet or number lists and change the numbering options for heading level styles. You can further select options to **AutoFormat** a document, browse and apply or modify **Styles**, set the properties of a **Frame**, or change the scaling and size of a **Picture**, or change the fill, line, size and position of a selected **Drawing Object**.

Tools   Produces a pull-down menu that gives access to **Spelling**, & **Grammar** checkers, the **Thesaurus**, and the **Hyphenation** option. It is from here that you can change the **Language** formatting of the selected characters, display the **Word Count** statistics of the current document, add or delete **AutoCorrect** entries, prepare for **Mail Merge**, or create and print **Envelopes and Labels**. Further, you can set **Revision** marking for the active document, and run, create, delete or revise a **Macro** (a set of instructions). Finally, you can **Customize** Word to your requirements and you can change various categories of Word for Windows **Options**.

Table   You can use the **Insert Table** option of the pull-down menu to create a table of specified rows and columns at the insertion point. Once a table exists, the rest of the options of the pull-down menu become available to you. From here you can **Insert Rows**, **Delete**, **Merge** and **Split Cells**, **Select** a **Row**, a **Column** or a **Table**. Further, you can select the **Table AutoFormat** option to choose from a set of pre-formatted table styles and have them applied to your table, change the **Cell Height and Width**, and toggle the table **headings** attribute on and off. Finally, you can select a section of text and use the **Convert Text to Table** option to have it incorporated within a table, rearrange a selection into a specified **Sort** order, insert a paragraph mark above the current table row by using the **Split Table** option, and toggle the table **Gridlines** on and off.

Window   Produces a menu to open a **New Window**, and control the display of existing open windows on the screen.

Help   Activates the help menu which you can use
to access the help **Index**, select the **Quick
Preview**, **Examples and Demos**, or **Tip of
the Day**, or get **WordPerfect** user help and
information on **Technical Support**.

Shortcut Menus:

New to version 6 are context-sensitive shortcut menus. If you
click the right mouse button on any screen, or document, a
shortcut menu is displayed with the most frequently used
commands relating to the type of work you were doing at the
time.

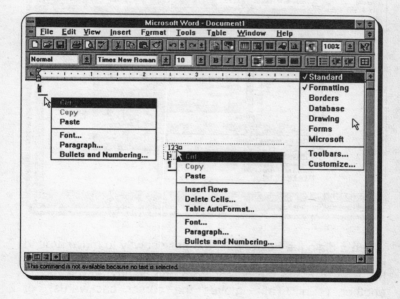

The composite screen dump above shows in turn the shortcut
menus that open when the editing area is selected, a table is
selected, or either of the Toolbars is selected.

So, whatever you are doing in Word 6, you have rapid
access to a menu of relevant functions by right clicking your
mouse. Left clicking the mouse at a menu selection will
choose that function.

Dialogue Boxes:

Three periods after a sub-menu option or command, means that a dialogue box will open when the option or command is selected. A dialogue box is used for the insertion of additional information, such as the name of a file or path.

To see a dialogue box, press <Alt+F>, and select the **Open** option. The 'Open' dialogue box appears on the screen as follows:

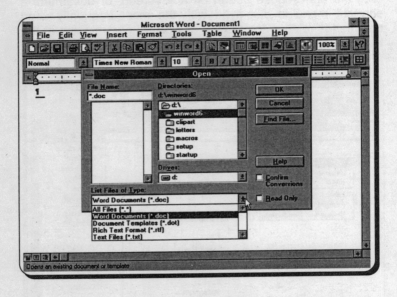

When a dialogue box opens, the easiest way to move around it is by clicking with the mouse, otherwise the <Tab> key can be used to move the cursor from one column in the box to another (<Shift+Tab> moves the cursor backwards), or alternatively you can move directly to a desired field by holding the <Alt> key down and pressing the underlined letter in the field name. Within a column of options you must use the arrow keys to move from one to another. Having selected an option or typed in information, you must press a command button such as the **OK** or **Cancel** button, or choose from additional options. To select the **OK** button with the mouse, simply point and click, while with the keyboard you must first

24

press the <Tab> key until the dotted rectangle moves to the required button, and then press the <Enter> key. Pressing <Enter> at any time while a dialogue box is open, will cause the marked items to be selected and the box to be closed.

Some dialogue boxes contain List boxes which show a column of available choices (similar to the one at the bottom of the previous screen dump which appeared by pressing the down-arrow button). If there are more choices than can be seen in the area provided, use the scroll bars to reveal them. To select a single item from a List box, either double-click the item, or use the arrow keys to highlight the item and press <Enter>. Other dialogue boxes contain Option buttons with a list of mutually exclusive items. The default choice is marked with a black dot against its name, while unavailable options are dimmed. Other dialogue boxes contain Check boxes which offer a list of options you can switch on or off. Selected options show a cross in the box against the option name.

To cancel a dialogue box, either press the **Cancel** button, or press the <Esc> key. Pressing the <Esc> key in succession, closes one dialogue box at a time, and eventually aborts the menu option.

The Formatting Bar:

This is located below the Toolbar at the top of the Word for Windows screen and is divided into seven sections, as shown below. These can only be accessed by clicking on them with the left mouse button.

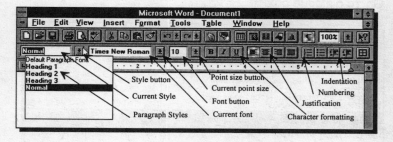

The Current Style box on the left of the Character formatting buttons, shows the style of the current paragraph; the one containing the cursor. By clicking the down-arrow button next to it, a list of all the available styles in the active template is produced (as shown). Clicking on one of these will change the style of the current paragraph.

To the right of the Style button is the Current font box which shows the current typeface. Clicking on the down-arrow button to the right of it allows you to change the typeface of any selected text. The Current point size box shows the size of selected characters. This size can be changed by clicking on the down-arrow button next to it and selecting another size from the displayed list.

Next, are three Character formatting buttons which allow you to enhance selected text by emboldening, italicising, or underlining it. The next four buttons allow you to change the justification of a selected paragraph, while the next four help you set the different types of Numbering and Indentation options. The last button allows you to add borders and shading to selected paragraphs, table cells and frames.

The Status Bar:

This is located at the bottom of the Word window and is used to display statistics about the active document. For example, when a document is being opened, the Status bar displays for a short time its name and length in terms of total number of characters. Once a document is opened, the Status bar displays the statistics of the document at the insertion point; here it is on Page 2, Section 1, 1 character from the left margin. Double-clicking the left of the status bar displays the Go To dialogue box.

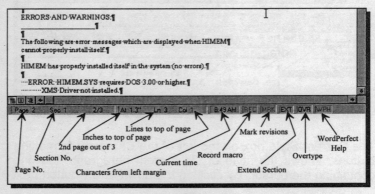

26

3. THE WINDOWS ENVIRONMENT

The Mouse Pointers

As with all other graphical based programs the use of a mouse makes many operations both easier and more fun to carry out.

Word has several different mouse pointers (similar to those found in Windows 3.1 or higher), as illustrated below, which it uses for its various functions. When the program is initially started up the first you will see is the hourglass, which turns into a large I-beam when the pointer is over your text editing area. As soon as the pointer is moved over the borders, menus or dialogue boxes it changes to an upward pointing hollow arrow. In the selection bar area, the pointer slants to the right.

 The hourglass which displays when you are waiting while Word is performing a function.

 The I-beam which appears in normal text areas of the screen.

 The arrow which appears when the pointer is placed over menus, scrolling bars, and buttons.

 The slanted arrow which appears when the pointer is placed in the selection bar area of text or a table.

 The move arrow which appears when drag-moving text.

 The frame cross which you drag to create a frame.

 The 4-headed arrow used to move a frame.

 The large 4-headed arrow which appears after choosing the **Control, Move/Size** command(s) for moving or sizing windows.

⇕ ⤢
⤡ ⇔   Double arrows which appear when over the border of a window, or the side of a frame, used to drag the side and alter the size of the window, or frame.

≑   The split box which appears when you select the **Control, Split** command, or when the mouse pointer is on the split box in the vertical scroll bar.

◄‖►   The vertical split arrow which appears when pointing on the vertical separation of cells in a table, and used to change the width of table columns.

↓   The vertical pointer which appears when pointing over a column in a table and used to select the column.

⌐ᵐ   The Help hand which appears in the help windows, and is used to access 'hypertext' type links.

⪢?   The query pointer which appears on the screen after you click the Help button on the Tool bar. Pointing to a command name or an area on the screen and clicking allows you to view a Help topic relating to the selected item.

Manipulating Windows

Word for Windows allows the display of multiple documents, like any other Windows application. Each of these documents displays on the screen in its own window, which can be full screen size, part screen size, or reduced to an icon. Further, each window can be subdivided into panes.

To use any Windows program effectively, you will need to be able to manipulate a series of windows, to select which one is to be active, to move them, or change their size, so that you can see all the relevant parts of each one. What follows is a short discussion on how to manipulate windows.

Changing the Active Window:

To select the active window amongst those displayed on the screen, point to it and click the left mouse button, or, if you are in full screen mode, choose the **Window** option of the main menu and select the appropriate number of the window you want to make the active one.

Moving Windows and Dialogue Boxes:

When you have multiple windows or dialogue boxes on the screen, you might want to move a particular one to a different part of the screen. This can be achieved with either the mouse or the keyboard, but not if the window occupies the full screen, for obvious reasons.

To move a window, or a dialogue box, with the mouse, point to the title bar and drag it (press the left button and keep it pressed while moving the mouse) until the shadow border is where you want it to be, then release the mouse button.

To move a window with the keyboard, press <Alt+Spacebar> to reveal the Application Control menu, or <Alt+–> to reveal the Document Control menu. Then, press **M** to select **Move** which causes a four-headed arrow to appear in the title bar and use the arrow keys to move the shadow border of the window to the required place. Press <Enter> to fix the window to its new position or <Esc> to cancel the relocation.

Sizing a Window:

You can change the size of a window with either the mouse or the keyboard. To size an active window with the mouse, move the window so that the side you want to change is visible, then move the mouse pointer to the edge of the window or corner so that it changes to a two-headed arrow, then drag the two-headed arrow in the direction you want that side or corner to move. Continue dragging until the shadow border is the size you require, then release the mouse button.

To size a window with the keyboard, press either <Alt+Spacebar> or <Alt+–> to reveal the Application Control menu or the Document Control menu, then press **S** to select **Size** which causes the four-headed arrow to appear. Now press the arrow key that corresponds to the edge you want to move, or if a corner, press the two arrow keys (one after the other) corresponding to the particular corner, which causes the pointer to change to a two-headed arrow. Press an appropriate arrow key in the direction you want that side or corner to move and continue to do so until the shadow border is the size you require, then press <Enter> to fix the new window size.

Minimising and Maximising Windows:

Word can be minimised into an icon at the bottom of the screen. This can be done either by using the mouse to click at the 'Minimise' button (the downward arrow in the upper-right corner of the window), or by pressing <Alt+Spacebar> or <Alt+–> to reveal the Application Control menu or the Document Control menu, and selecting **n** for **Minimise**.

To maximise a window so that it fills the entire screen, either click on the 'maximise' button (the upward arrow in the upper-right corner of the window), or press <Alt+Spacebar> or <Alt+–> to display the Application Control menu or the Document Control menu, and select **x** for **Maximise**.

An application which has been minimised or maximised can be returned to its original size and position on the screen by either double clicking on its icon to expand it to a window, or clicking on the double-headed button in the upper-right corner of the maximised window to reduce it to its former size. With the keyboard, press <Alt+Spacebar> to display the Application Control menu, or <Alt+–> to display the Document Control menu, and select **R** for **Restore**.

Closing a Window

A document window can be closed at any time to save screen space and memory. To do this, either double-click on the Control menu button (the large hyphen in the upper-left corner of the window, or press <Alt+–> and select **c** for **Close** from the Control menu.

If you have made any changes to a document since the last time you saved it, Word will warn you with the appearance of a dialogue box asking confirmation prior to closing it.

Windows Display Arrangement

In Windows' Program Manager, you can display multiple windows in both tiled and cascaded (overlapping) forms - the choice being a matter of balance between personal preference and the type of work you are doing at the time.

In Word for Windows, multiple documents are only displayed automatically in tile form, but you could rearrange them. To illustrate the point, select the **File, New** command twice; each time you select this command, the following dialogue box appears on the screen:

This 'New' dialogue box, which will be discussed in more detail later, is used to select the template to be used with a new document. In this case the default 'Normal' template is fine, therefore accept it by pressing <Enter>, or by clicking the **OK** button. When Document3 is displayed on screen, select the **Window, Arrange All** command. The three opened windows then rearrange themselves in tile form, as shown below.

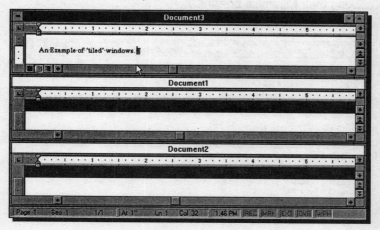

Now try to arrange these windows in cascade form by re-sizing them and moving them so they appear as follows:

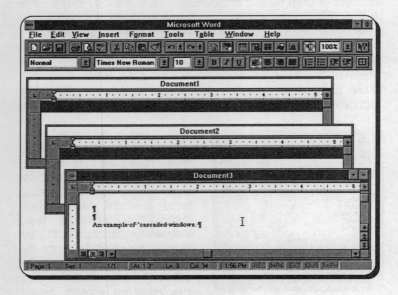

Next, try arranging the three windows as shown below. To do this, you will need to reduce two of the documents to icons by clicking their Minimise buttons.

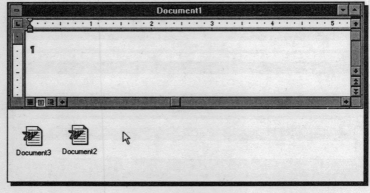

When you are learning Word for Windows, it is very easy to open more files or documents than you need. Unless you check with the **Window** command, you may not even know that some of these files or documents are open. Unfortunately the program does not have the option of closing the active window (the one whose title bar is highlighted) when a new one is opened.

We recommend you check every now and then and, to conserve memory, close any unwanted files, or documents, by first making them active, then using the **File, Close** command. The other easy way to close a file is to double-click the left mouse button on the document control box as described earlier in the chapter. This is at the left end of the menu bar if the document is set to full page, or at the left end of the document title bar, if it is windowed.

The Windows Control Panel

The Control Panel provides a quick and easy way to change the hardware and software settings of your system. For the sake of completeness we describe its use at this point.

Access to the Control Panel, from Word involves returning to the Windows Program Manager. The quickest way to do this is by repeatedly pressing the <Tab> key with the <Alt> key held down; this cycles through any running applications. When the Program Manager box shows on the screen, release the <Alt> key to make it the active application.

Another way to perform the same application change, makes use of the Word (or the Application) Control Menu which is opened when the upper Control box is clicked on.

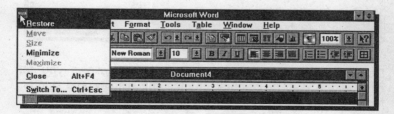

Select **Switch To** from this menu to open the Task List dialogue box, shown on the next page. This gives a listing of all the applications that are currently running under Windows.

Select the Program Manager option and click on the **Switch To** button. The other buttons in this box allow you to

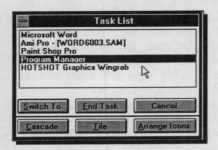

manipulate and close the running application windows and to arrange any icons at the bottom of the screen.

Once in the Program Manager window, you can normally find the Control Panel icon, shown below, in the Main group window.

Double-clicking on this icon will open the Control Panel window from which the various Control Panel options can be accessed.

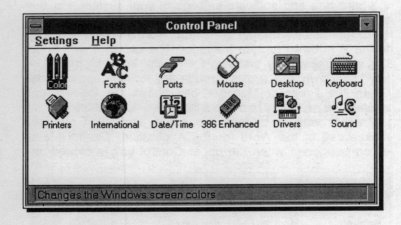

Double-clicking at the Control Panel icons allows you to change the display colours, change the display and printer fonts, specify parameters for any serial ports installed on your system, change the settings of your mouse, change the appearance of your display, specify resource allocations when running in 386 mode, install and configure your printer(s), specify international settings, such as the

formatting of numbers and dates, change the keyboard
repeat rate, change the date and time of your system, and
specify whether Windows should beep when it detects an
error.

All of these features control the environment in which the
Word package operates and you should become familiar with
them.

Checking the Windows Printer Set-up:

When Windows was first installed on your computer the
printers you intend to use with your Windows applications
should have been selected, and the SETUP program should
have installed the appropriate printer drivers. Before printing
for the first time with Word, you would be wise to ensure that

your printer is in fact properly installed. To do this,
double-click on the 'Printers' icon in the Windows
Control Panel, shown here, which causes the
following Printers dialogue box to be opened.

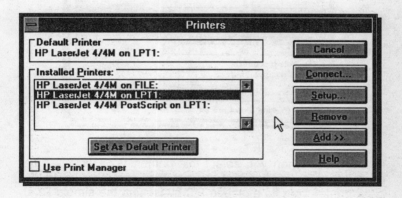

Here, two printer drivers have been installed. An HP LaserJet
4/4M as the 'default' (the printer's name is highlighted and it
also appears in the Default Printer box), configured to print to
the parallel printer port LPT1, and an HP LaserJet 4/4M
PostScript, also configured to print to the parallel printer port.
The first printer has also been configured for output to a disc
file. Obviously, your selections will not be the same.

Any of the other installed printers can be made the default by highlighting its name and pressing the **Set As Default Printer** button. The **Setup** button allows you to select the size of paper and orientation of printout (portrait or landscape).

Best printed output results are obtained when using a laser printer. So, if you want to produce high quality documents, and you have access to a laser printer (even if it is not connected to your computer and does not itself have access to Word), then install the laser printer as an additional printer to be used with Windows and configure it to print to 'File'. To do this, first select the printer in the 'Printers' dialogue box, click the **Connect** button to open the dialogue box displayed below and select **File:** from the list of available printer **Ports**.

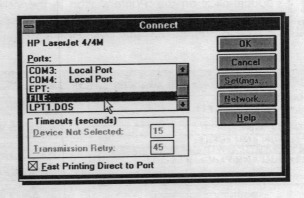

In the future when you select this printer, your work will be printed to a file on disc and you can then copy that file to the laser printer from its attached PC by issuing the simple DOS command

```
COPY Filename LPT1: /B
```

The /B switch in this command tells the printer to expect a binary file; without this the process may, or may not work. So it is safer to use it.

To install a different printer, press the **Add** button in the 'Printers' dialogue box, choose a printer from the list displayed, and select **Install**. Each time you choose to install a different printer, Windows will ask you to insert a particular Windows disc in drive A:, so that the appropriate driver can be copied on to your hard disc.

Using Help in Word

Using the Microsoft Windows Help Program, Word provides on-line Help for every function. You can re-size, move, tile, or cascade the Help window and the current document so that you can keep both of them displayed at the same time.

Help topics can be printed on paper by selecting the topic, then using Help's **File, Print Topic** command, as shown below:

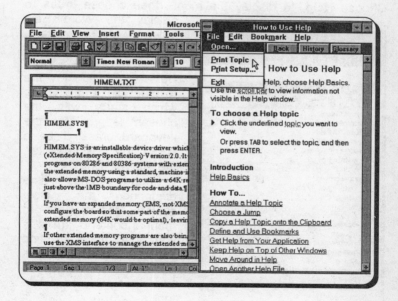

You can even copy and edit text from the Help windows into a document by using Help's **Edit, Copy** command, to copy selected text to the Clipboard.

There are several ways to obtain on-line Help:

On-line Help Messages:
Word displays a command description in the Status bar when you choose a menu or command.

Context Sensitive Help:
Simply press **F1** to get instant help on any menu function that you are carrying out. If you are not using a menu box you will bring up the Help Contents window. Selecting the **File, Exit** command (<Alt+F> followed by X), will close the Help window and return you to your original screen. The <Alt+F4> quick key combination may also be used to exit Help.

Help Menu:
Choose **Help**, to display the menu, then choose **Index** to

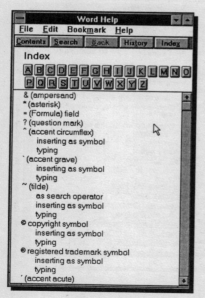

display the Word Help Index shown here. Pressing one of the letter buttons, causes Word Help to jump to the relevant part of the listing which starts with the chosen letter. With the keyboard, press <Tab> to select the desired letter, then press <Enter>.

Spend some time exploring the Help system. Most of the Word manual contents are in it; you just have to find them. Many Help topics contain cross-references to other related Help topics, which display in green. These are often known as 'hypertext' links, and clicking the hand pointer on them displays their content.

4. WORD DOCUMENT BASICS

When the program is first used, all Word's features default to those shown on page 15. It is quite possible to use Word in this mode, without changing any main settings, but as we work through the next two chapters we will explore some of the package's very powerful features, which will allow you to do much more than just the basics.

Entering Text:

Before going any further start Word, if necessary, and type the memo displayed below into a new document. The text may not be relevant to you, but it will give us a chance to illustrate some of Word's capabilities.

As you type in text, any time you want to force a new line, or paragraph, just press <Enter>. While typing within a paragraph, Word sorts out line lengths automatically, without you having to press any keys to move to a new line. This is known as 'word wrap'. If you make a mistake while typing, press the <BkSp> key enough times to erase the mistake and type the text again. At this stage, don't worry if the length of the lines below differ from those on your display.

MEMO TO PC USERS
Personal Computers
The microcomputers in the DP room are a mixture of
IBM PS/2s with 3.5" drives of 1.44MB capacity, IBM
ATs with 5.25" high density drives of 1.2MB capacity,
and some IBM compatible machines with both 3.5" and
5.25" drives, which are connected to various printers. In
this way, no matter which type of machine you use, saved
documents on discs of either size can be printed.

The computer you are using will have at least a 40MB
hard disc on which a number of software packages have
been installed. To make life easier, the hard disc is highly
structured with each package installed in a separate
directory. When the computer is first switched on, the
following prompt is displayed on your screen:

C:\>

If you want to type text indented from the left margin (like the last entry of the text below), use the <Tab> key before typing the information. Word has tab stops at every half inch by default. Formatting with tabs will be discussed later on.

Styles:

As you can see at the extreme left of the Formatting bar, the Style Status box contains the word **Normal**. This means that all the text you have entered is, at the moment, shown in the Normal style which is one of the styles available in the NORMAL template. As mentioned previously, every document produced by Word has to use a template. By default the template NORMAL is used and at this stage we will not change this. The template contains, both the document page settings and a set of formatting instructions which can be rapidly applied to paragraphs within a document.

To demonstrate this, let's reformat our rather boring looking memo, but first, select the **File, Page Setup** command, click the left mouse button at the **Paper Size** tab on the displayed dialogue box and click the down-arrow against the **Paper Size** box to reveal the list of available paper sizes. Next, change the page size from Letter (the standard American page size) to A4 (the standard British page size), as shown below, then press the **Default** button and confirm that you wish this change to affect all new documents based on the NORMAL template.

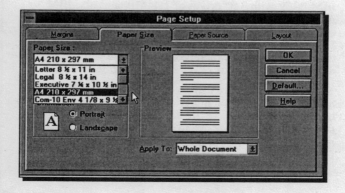

Now, place the cursor (insertion pointer) on the title line of the memo, left click the Style Status button, and select the **Heading 1** style. The title line reformats instantly in bold, and in Arial typeface of point size 14. With the cursor in the second line of text select **Heading 3** which reformats the line in bold, and Times New Roman point size 12. Your memo should look quite presentable now, as shown below.

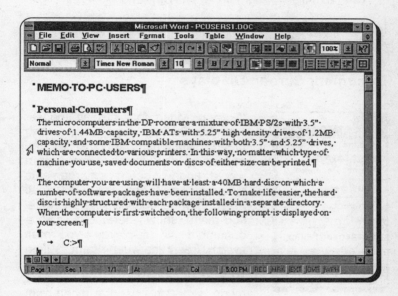

Moving Around a Document:
You can move the cursor around a document with the normal direction keys, and with the key combinations shown below:

To move	Press
Left one character	←
Right one character	→
Up one line	↑
Down one line	↓
Left one word	Ctrl+←
Right one word	Ctrl+→
To beginning of line	Home
To end of line	End

To paragraph beginning	Ctrl+↑
To paragraph end	Ctrl+↓
Up one screen	PgUp
Down one screen	PgDn
To top of previous page	Ctrl+PgUp
To top of next page	Ctrl+PgDn
To beginning of file	Ctrl+Home
To end of file	Ctrl+End

In a multi-page document, use the **Edit**, **Go To** command (or <Ctrl+G>), to jump to a specified page number.

Document Screen Displays

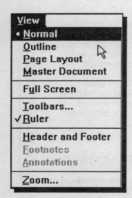

Word provides four display modes, Normal, Outline, Page Layout, and Master Document, as well as the options to view your documents in a whole range of screen enlargements by selecting **Zoom**. You control all these viewing options with the **View** sub-menu, shown here, and when a document is displayed you can switch freely between them. When first loaded the screen displays in Normal mode. To select another mode, simply choose the mode from the **View** sub-menu.

Normal Mode:

Normal mode returns you to normal viewing from either Outline or Page Layout viewing mode.

Outline Mode:

Outline mode provides a collapsible view of a document, which enables you to see its organisation at a glance. You can display all the text in a file, or just the text that uses the paragraph styles you specify. Using the Outline mode, allows you to quickly rearrange large sections of text.

Some people like to create an outline of their document first, consisting of all the headings, then to sort out the document structure and finally fill in the text. Outline mode is ideal for this type of working method.

Page Layout Mode:

Layout mode provides a WYSIWYG (what you see is what you get) view of a document. The text displays in the typefaces and point sizes you specify, and with the selected attributes (alignment, indention, spacing, etc.).

All frames, tables, graphics, headers, footers, and footnotes appear on the screen as they will in the final printed document.

Master Document Mode:

This document mode provides you with an outline view of a document that takes its contents from one or more Word documents. For example, if you are writing a book, you could make each chapter a sub-document of such a Master Document. The Master Document could then be used to reorganise, add or remove sub-documents.

When you select the Master Document mode, Word automatically displays the Master Document and Outline toolbars.

Different Document Views

With Word you can select to view your document in **Full Screen**, in which case the Toolbars, Ruler, Scroll bars, and Status bar are removed, presenting you with a clean, uncluttered screen. To return to the usual Word screen, click at the 'Full' icon, shown here, which appears at the bottom of your screen when in this mode.

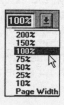

Normally Word shows the screen page in the same size as other Microsoft Windows applications with a **Zoom** magnification factor of 100%. You can change this by clicking the 'Zoom Control' icon on the Tool bar. Clicking its down arrow button, reveals other magnification factors, as shown here.

43

You can also control the view of your document by selecting **View**, **Zoom** command and select a setting in the 'Zoom' dialogue box shown below:

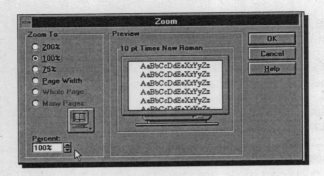

From here you can specify a percentage size between **75%** and **200%**, where **100%** represents the standard view. The default is set as 100%. Once you are happy about controlling this view it is the one you will probably be most comfortable working with.

The 200% view doubles the size of the standard view and allows you to zoom quickly to a portion of a page so that you can see fine details of your layout. This view is also fully editable and is most useful when using very small fonts.

Other options are available: **Page Width** reduces or enlarges the display of a document so that it fits within the left and right margins, **Whole Page** (only available if the **File, Print Preview** command is selected first) reduces the display so that the margins of the displayed section fit within the document window, and **Many Pages** (also only available if the **File, Print Preview** command is selected first) allows you to see two or more pages in print preview mode. With the last two options, you may not be able to read all your document's text, but it can be very useful for checking on the layout of your pages, or for getting a rough overview of the document.

Finally, the **Percent** option reduces or enlarges the display of the document by the specified percentage, which must be between 10% and 200%.

Display Screen Options:

You can choose to display certain parts of the Word window and hide other parts by selectively switching off the **Toolbars**, **Ruler**, **Header/Footer**, **Footnotes**, and **Annotations** by clicking at the relevant **View** sub-menu options. You can do this in most modes and views, with unavailable options in certain modes being shown dimmed.

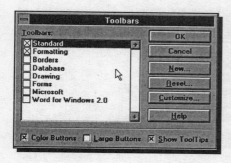

Selecting **Toolbars** displays the dialogue box, shown here, from which you can control further options, such as the type of 'Borders' in your document, and/or which other bars should be displayed on your screen.

If you turn off everything (not as drastic as selecting **Full Screen**), you will be left with a screen which almost looks like a blank piece of paper, but for the Menu bar, Status bar and Scroll bars. By default, the **Toolbars**, and **Ruler** are switched on.

If you operate much with a clearer screen or **Full Screen**, you will need to learn the keyboard shortcuts for commands (see Appendix A). These give you access to most of the more common menu commands without having to open the menu bars or return to 'Full Screen'.

We leave it to you now to have fun exploring the different modes and views available in Word.

Changing Default Options

You can change the default options available to you in Word for Windows, by selecting the **Tools, Options** command, to obtain the dialogue box shown on the next page. In this you can specify the default **View** options (what is displayed first), adjust the **General** Word settings, adjust the **Print** settings, change the **Save** options, and many others. In what follows, we only discuss the above four options.

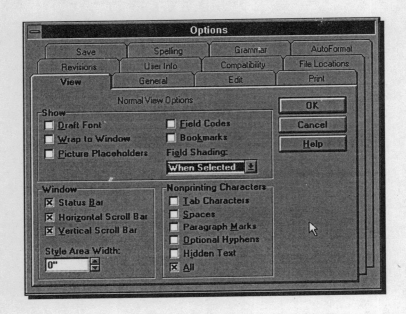

It is from this View dialogue box that you can change the way your current View option is displayed, the way text is shown, what appears in the document window (you could, for example, selectively switch off the Scroll bars and the Status bar), and whether non-printing characters, such as Tabs, Spaces, and Paragraph marks, are shown or not.

Finally, if you select the **Draft Font** option (Normal and Outline views only), Word displays a less formatted view of your document. Text with attributes and enhancements appears underlined, and pictures or objects are not displayed in their frames. The advantage of selecting **Draft Font** is that you can edit a document very quickly, as the amount of computations required to display text in this mode are reduced to a minimum, therefore speeding up the whole process.

When you have finished with the 'View' options, you can click the **General** tab of the Options dialogue box, to obtain a similar dialogue box to the one above, but with a new set of options (shown on the next page) available to you for adjustment.

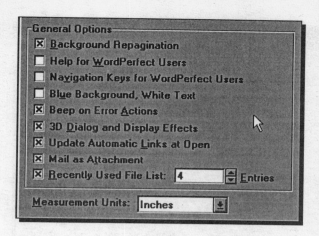

From here you can change several options, including the colour of text and its background, the number of files used in the File List at the end of the **File** sub-menu, and the units of measure from inches, centimetres, points, or Picas.

To adjust the printing options, click the **Print** tab of the Options dialogue box, which causes the following set of options to be displayed:

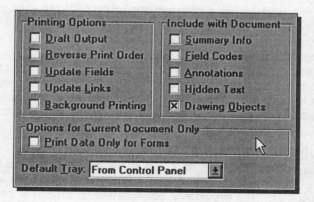

From here you can select various print options, including the **Draft Output** mode, and the **Reverse Print Order** mode, or choose to print the **Summary Info** or **Annotations** when printing your document.

Finally, clicking the **Save** tab of the Options dialogue box, displays the following set of options:

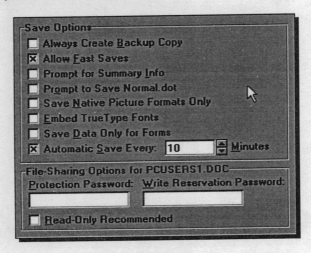

From here you can select the **Always Create Backup Copy** option for your work, or enable **Automatic Save Every** and specify how often. This last save option can be dangerous if you are working on a detailed document, change your mind and need to return to the original form, only to find it has been replaced. We find it far safer to manually save our work at regular intervals.

If you don't like to be prompted for summary information for your newly created document, you could disable this option from within this dialogue box, so that it does not appear on the screen when you first try to save your document to disc.

Saving to a File

To save a document to disc, use either the **File, Save** or **File, Save As** command. The **File, Save** command is used when a document has previously been saved to disc in a named file; using the command automatically saves your work under the existing filename without prompting you. The **File, Save As** command is used when you want to save your document with a different name from the one you gave it already.

Using the **File, Save As** command (or the very first time you use the **File, Save** command when a document has no name). causes the following dialogue box to appear on your screen:

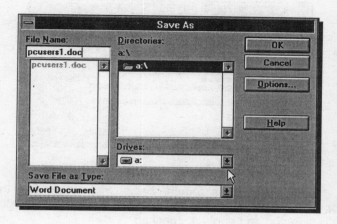

Note that the old document name is highlighted in the **File Name** field box and the program is waiting for you to type a new name. Any name you type (don't use more than 8 characters and don't bother to type the .doc extension as the program adds it automatically) will replace the existing document name.

You can select a drive other than the one displayed, by clicking the down arrow against the **Drives** field. To save your work currently in memory, move the cursor into the **File Name** box, and type PCUSERS1.

By using the **Save File as Type** button we could have saved the Document Template, or the Text Only parts of our work, or we could have saved our document in a variety of other formats, such as DOS Text, ASCII, Rich Text Format, or a number of WordPerfect, Word for Windows, and Word for DOS formats, as well as in Excel and Windows Write formats. All these different formats are saved with appropriate extensions which are recognised by the packages in question.

A useful feature in Word is the facility to add a document description to every file by selecting the **File, Summary Info** command. A box, as shown below, opens for you to type additional information about your document.

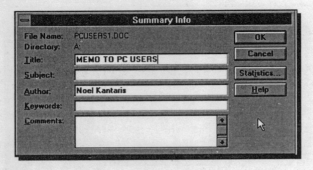

To do this on a more regular basis, make sure that the **Prompt for Summary Info** box in the Save Options dialogue box is selected and appears checked.

Closing a Document:

There are several ways to close a document in Word. Once you have saved it you can double click on the Document Control button at the left end of the menu bar; you would usually use this method when you have several files open together.

If you want to open a new, or another, document you could first use the **File, Close** command to close the current document (remove it from your computer's memory) before using either the **New** or the **Open** options of the **File** menu. If the document has changed since the last time it was saved, you will be given the option to save it before it is removed from memory.

If a document is not closed before a new document is opened, then both documents will be held in memory, but only one will be the current document. To find out which documents are held in memory, use the **Window** command to reveal the following drop down menu:

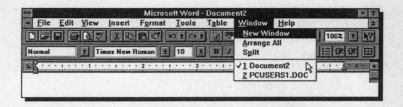

In this case, the first document in the list is the current document, and to make another document the current one, either type the document number, or point at its name and click the left mouse button.

To close a document which is not the current document, use the **Window** command, make it current, and then use the **File, Close** command.

5. EDITING YOUR DOCUMENTS

It will not be long, when using Word, before you will need to edit your document. This could include deleting unwanted words, correcting a mistake or adding extra text in the document. All these operations are very easy to carry out.

For small deletions, such as letters or words, the easiest method to adopt is the use of the <Del> or <BkSp> keys. With the <Del> key, position the cursor on the first letter you want to delete and press <Del>; the letter is deleted and the following text moves one space to the left. With the <BkSp> key, position the cursor immediately to the right of the character to be deleted and press <BkSp>; the cursor moves one space to the left pulling the rest of the line with it and overwriting the character to be deleted. Note that the difference between the two is that with <Del> the cursor does not move at all.

Word processing is usually carried out in the insert mode. Any characters typed will be inserted at the cursor location (insertion point) and the following text will be pushed to the right, and down, to make room. To insert blank lines in your text, place the cursor at the beginning of the line where the blank line is needed and press <Enter>. To remove the blank line, position the cursor at its leftmost end and press <Del>.

When larger scale editing is needed you have several alternatives with Word. You can use the **Cut, Copy** and **Paste** operations, after first 'selecting' the text to be altered. These functions are then available when the **Edit** sub-menu is activated. Instead of using the sub-menu you can click on Toolbar button alternatives for all the editing commands. This makes working with a mouse very much easier and quicker. A method, new to later versions of Word is to use the 'drag' facility for copying or moving text.

Selecting Text

The procedure in Word, as with most Windows based applications, is first to select the text to be altered before any operation, such as formatting or editing, can be carried out on it. Selected text is highlighted on the screen. This can be carried out in two main ways:

A. Using the keyboard, to select:

- A block of text.

  Position the cursor on the first character to be selected and hold down the <Shift> key while using the arrow keys to highlight the required text, then release the <Shift> key.

- From the present cursor position to the end of the line.

  Use <Shift+End>.

- From the present cursor position to the beginning of the line.

  Use <Shift+Home>.

- From the present cursor position to the end of the document.

  Use <Shift+Ctrl+End>.

- From the present cursor position to the beginning of the document.

  Use <Shift+Ctrl+Home>.

B. With the mouse, to select:

- A block of text.

  Press down the left mouse button at the beginning of the block and while holding it pressed, drag the cursor across the block so that the desired text is highlighted, then release the mouse button.

- A word.

  Double-click at the word.

54

Deleting Blocks of Text

When text is 'cut' it is removed from the document, but placed on the clipboard until further text is either copied or cut. With Word any selected text can be deleted by pressing **Edit, Cut,** or by pressing the <Del>, or <BkSp> keys. However, using **Edit, Cut**, allows you to use the **Edit, Paste** command, but using the <Del> or <BkSp> keys, does not.

The Undo Command

As text is lost with the delete command you should use it with caution, but if you do make a mistake all is not lost as long as you act promptly. The **Edit, Undo** command or <Ctrl+Z> (or <Alt+BkSp>) reverses your most recent editing or formatting commands.

You can also use the Tool bar buttons, shown here, to undo one of several editing or formatting mistakes (press the 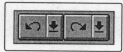 down arrow to the right of the left button to see a list of your changes) or even redo any one of the undo moves with the right button.

Undo does not reverse any action once editing changes have been saved to file. Only editing done after the save can be reversed.

Finding and Changing Text

Word allows you to search for specifically selected text, or character combinations, using the **Find** or the **Replace** option from the **Edit** command sub-menu.

Using the **Find** option (<Ctrl+F>), will highlight each occurrence of the supplied text in turn so that you can carry out some action on it, such as change its font or appearance, while using the **Replace** option (<Ctrl+H>), allows you to specify what replacement is to be automatically carried out. For example, in a long article you may decide to replace every occurrence of the word 'microcomputers' with the word 'PCs'.

To illustrate the **Replace** procedure, either select the option from the **Edit** sub-menu or use the quick key combination <Ctrl+H>. This opens the Replace dialogue box, displayed on the top half of the composite screen dump shown below.

Towards the bottom of the dialogue box, there are four check boxes with which you can match the case of letters in the search string, and/or a whole word. The last two check boxes can be used for a pattern, or sounds like matching.

The two buttons, **Format** and **Special**, situated at the bottom of the dialogue box, let you control how the search is carried out. The lists of available options, when either of these buttons is pressed, are displayed in the above composite screen dump.

You can force both the search and the replace operations to work with exact text attributes. For example, selecting the **Font** option from the list under **Format**, displays a dialogue box in which you select font (such as Arial, Times New Roman, etc.), font-style (regular, bold, italic, etc.), underline options (single, double, etc.), and special effects (strike-through, superscript, subscript, etc.). Selecting the **Paragraph** option lets you control indentation, spacing (before and after), and alignment. Finally, by selecting **Style** you can search for, or replace, different paragraph styles. This can be useful if you develop a new style and want to change all the text of another style in a document to use it.

With the use of the **Special** button, you can search for, and replace, various specified document marks, tabs, hard returns, etc., or a combination of both these and text, as listed in the previous screen dump.

Advanced Search Operators:

The list below gives the key combinations of special characters to type into the **Find What** and **Replace With** boxes when the **Use Pattern Matching** box is checked.

Type	*To find or replace*
?	Any single character. For example, searching for nec?, will find such words as necessary, neck, nectar, connect, etc.
*	Any string of characters. For example, searching for c*r, will find such words as cellar, character, chillier, etc.
[ ]	One of the specified characters. For example, searching for d[oi]g, will find such words as dog and dig.
[-]	Any single character in the specified range. For example, searching for [b-f]ore, will find such words as bore, core, fore, etc.
[!]	Any single character except the character inside the brackets. For example, searching for l[!o]ve, will find live, but not love.

[!s-z]	Any single character except characters in the range inside the brackets. For example, searching for [!s-z]ong, will find long but not song.
{n}	Exactly n occurrences of the previous character. For example, searching for me{2}t, will find meet but not met.
{n,}	At least n occurrences of the previous character. For example, searching for me{1,}t, will find met and meet.
{n,m}	From n to m occurrences of the previous character. For example, searching for 9{1,3}, will find 9, 99, and 999.
@	One or more occurrences of the previous character. For example, searching for ro@t, will find rot and root.
<	The beginning of a word. For example, searching for <on, will find on and onto, but not upon.
>	The end of a word. For example, searching for >on, will find on and upon, but not onto.

Page Breaks

The program automatically inserts a 'soft' page break in a document when a page of typed text is full. To force a manual, or hard, page break in a document, either type <Ctrl+Enter> or use the **Insert**, **Break** command and select **Page Break** in the dialogue box, as shown below:

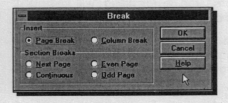

Pressing **OK** places a series of dots across the page to indicate the page break as shown overleaf. To delete manual page breaks place the cursor on the selection bar to the left of the page break mark, click once to highlight the line of dots, and press <Del>.

˙MEMO·TO·PC·USERS¶

˙Personal·Computers¶

The·microcomputers·in·the·DP·room·are·a·mixture·of·IBM·PS/2s·with·3.5"·
drives·of·1.44MB·capacity,·IBM·ATs·with·5.25"·high·density·drives·of·1.2MB·
capacity,·and·some·IBM·compatible·machines·with·both·3.5"·and·5.25"·drives,·
which·are·connected·to·various·printers.·In·this·way,·no·matter·which·type·of·
machine·you·use,·saved·documents·on·discs·of·either·size·can·be·printed.¶

¶
————————————————————— Page Break —————————————————————

The·computer·you·are·using·will·have·at·least·a·40MB·hard·disc·on·which·a·
number·of·software·packages·have·been·installed.·To·make·life·easier,·the·hard·
disc·is·highly·structured·with·each·package·installed·in·a·separate·directory.·
When·the·computer·is·first·switched·on,·the·following·prompt·is·displayed·on·
your·screen:¶

Soft page breaks which are automatically entered by the program at the end of lines, cannot be deleted.

Printing Documents

When Windows was first installed on your computer the printers you intend to use should have been selected, and the SETUP program should have installed the appropriate printer drivers. Before printing for the first time, you would be wise to ensure that your printer is in fact properly installed. To do this, open the Window's Control Panel, as described at the end of Chapter 3 and double click on the 'Printers' icon. This will open the **Printers** box shown below:

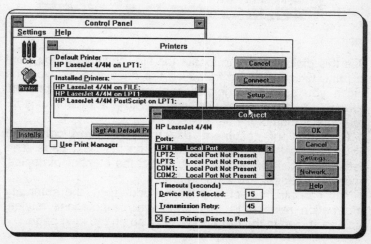

61

Here, two printer drivers have been installed; an HP LaserJet 4/4M as the 'default' printer configured to either output to a printer via the parallel port LPT1, or to a disc file, and an HP LaserJet 4/4M PostScript, also configured to output to a printer. Your selections may, obviously, not be the same. Should you need to change or add a new printer, refer to the end of Chapter 3.

Next, return to or reactivate Word and, if the document you want to print is not in memory, either click the 'Open' button on the Toolbar, or use the **File, Open** command, to display the Open dialogue box shown below.

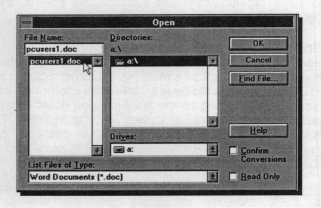

Use this dialogue box to locate the file (document) you want to print, which is to be found on the drive and directory on which you saved it originally, select it and press the **OK** button (or double-click its name), to load it into your computer's memory.

To print your document, use the **File, Print** command which opens the 'Print' box, shown on the next page. The settings in this box allow you to select the number of copies, and which pages, you want printed.

You can also select to print the document, the summary information relating to that document, annotations, styles, etc., as shown in the drop-down list also on the next page.

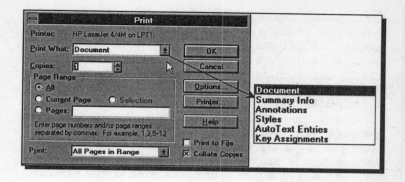

You can even change the selected printer by pressing the **Printer** button which displays the following dialogue box.

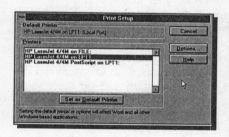

From this dialogue box you can select the default printer or any other installed printer. Pressing the **Options** button, displays the Setup dialogue box, shown below, which allows you to select the paper size, orientation needed, and printer resolution, etc.

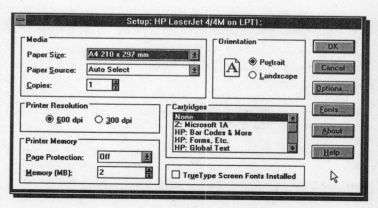

The **Options** button of the Setup dialogue box allows selection of graphics mode, graphics quality, and halftone options. The **Options** button on the Print dialogue box, on the other hand, gives you access to some more advanced print options, such as printing in reverse order, or with and without annotations, hidden text, field codes or document summary information.

Pressing the **OK** button on these various multi-level dialogue boxes, causes Word to accept your selections and return you to the previous level dialogue box, until the Print dialogue box is reached. Selecting **OK** on this first level dialogue box, sends print output from Word to your selection, either the printer connected to your computer, or to an encoded file on disc. Selecting **Cancel** on any level dialogue box, aborts the selections made at that level.

Do remember that, whenever you change printers, the appearance of your document may change, as Word uses the fonts available with the newly selected printer. This can affect the line lengths, which in turn will affect both the tabulation and pagination of your document.

Other enhancements of your document, such as selection of fonts, formatting of text, and pagination, will be discussed in the next two chapters.

6. FORMATTING YOUR WORK

Formatting involves the appearance of individual characters or words, the line spacing and alignment of paragraphs, and the overall page layout of the entire document. These functions are carried out in Word in several different ways. Primary page layout and text formatting can be included in Style Sheets and Templates, which will be discussed in Chapter 7. Within any document, however, you can override Paragraph Style formats by applying text formatting and enhancements manually to selected text. If you cancel this manual formatting by selecting the text and choosing, **Undo Formatting** (<Ctrl+Z>) from the **Edit** sub-menu, the text will revert to its original format.

Formatting Text:

The fonts available in Word depend on the printer(s) you have set-up in Microsoft Windows and selected in Word with the **File**, **Print, Printer** command. With Windows you can have fonts that display on your screen but that your printer cannot print, and vice versa.

If you select a printer font for which there is no exact screen font, then Word will select the nearest one that is available to display your work. Similarly, if the font selected is not available to your printer, Word will select the nearest one you do have available and will use that when printing. You might choose to do the latter, because you plan to print on a different printer from the one attached to your system. When you open your document on the computer that has the specified font, Word will display and print your document with the correct font.

Originally, the title of the memo PCUSERS1, which we created in Chapter 4, was typed in the 14 point size Arial typeface, while the subtitle and the main text were typed in 12 and 10 point size Times New Roman, respectively.

To change this memo into what appears on the screen dump displayed on the next page, first select the title of the memo and format it to bold, italics, 18 point size Arial and centre it between the margins, then select the subtitle and format it to bold, 14 point size Times New Roman.

Finally select each paragraph of the main body of the memo in turn, and format it to 12 point size Times New Roman. All of this formatting can be achieved by using the buttons on the Formatting Toolbar (see section 'Paragraph Alignment').

If you can't access these font styles, it will probably be because your printer does not support them, in which case you will need to select other fonts that are supported. Save the result under the new filename PCUSERS2.

MEMO·TO·PC·USERS¶

·Personal·Computers¶

The·microcomputers·in·the·DP·room·are·a·mixture·of·IBM·PS/2s·with·3.5"· drives·of·1.44MB·capacity,·IBM·ATs·with·5.25"·high·density·drives·of·1.2MB· capacity,·and·some·IBM·compatible·machines·with·both·3.5"·and·5.25"·drives,· which·are·connected·to·various·printers.·In·this·way,·no·matter·which·type·of· machine·you·use,·saved·documents·on·discs·of·either·size·can·be·printed.¶
¶
The·computer·you·are·using·will·have·at·least·a·40MB·hard·disc·on·which·a· number·of·software·packages·have·been·installed.·To·make·life·easier,·the·hard· disc·is·highly·structured·with·each·package·installed·in·a·separate·directory.· When·the·computer·is·first·switched·on,·the·following·prompt·is·displayed·on· your·screen:¶
¶
   → C:>¶

Some Font Basics:

A 'point' is a unit of measurement, approximately 1/72 of an inch, that determines the height of a character. There is another unit of character measurement called the 'pitch' which is the number of characters that can fit horizontally in one inch. The spacing of a font is either 'fixed' (monospaced) or 'proportional'. With fixed spacing, each character takes up exactly the same space, while proportionally spaced characters take up different spacing (an 'i' or a 't' take up less space than a 'u' or a 'w'). Thus the length of proportionally spaced text can vary depending on which letters it contains. However, numerals take up the same amount of space whether they have been specified as fixed or proportional.

Which fonts you choose is largely dependent on your printer, as mentioned previously. Windows 3.1 makes available several 'TrueType' fonts which can be used by Windows applications, such as Word. TrueType fonts are scaleable to any point size and look exactly the same on the screen as they do when printed.

In Word all manual formatting, including the selection of font, point size, style (bold, italic, strike-through, hidden and capitals), colour, super/subscript, and various underlines, are carried out by first selecting the text and then executing the formatting command. One method of activating formatting commands is through the **Fo̲rmat**, **F̲ont** command which displays the dialogue box shown below.

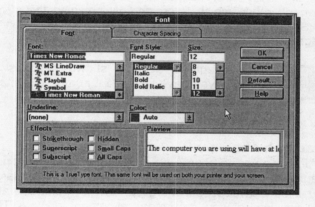

Another method is by using quick keys, as shown below.

Text Formatting with Quick Keys:
To format selected text, use the following shortcut keys.

To Format	*Type*
Bold	Ctrl+B
Italic	Ctrl+I
Underline	Ctrl+U
Word underline	Ctrl+Shift+W
Double underline	Ctrl+Shift+D

Subscript	Ctrl+=
Superscript	Ctrl+Shift+=
Small caps	Ctrl+Shift+K
All caps	Ctrl+Shift+A
Change case letters	Shift+F3
Hide text	Ctrl+Shift+H
Copy formats	Ctrl+Shift+C
Paste formats	Ctrl+Shift+V
Remove formats	Ctrl+Space
Next larger font size	Ctrl+>
Next smaller font size	Ctrl+<

Text Enhancements

Word defines a paragraph, as any text which is followed by a paragraph mark, which is created by pressing the <Enter> key. So single line titles, as well as long typed text, can form paragraphs.

 The paragraph symbol, shown here, is only visible if you have selected it from the Formatting Toolbar.

Paragraph Alignment:

Word allows you to align a paragraph at the left margin (the default), at the right margin, centred between both margins, or justified between both margins. As with most operations there are several ways to perform alignment in Word. These are as follows:

a. Using buttons on the **Formatting Toolbar**,
b. Using keyboard short cuts, when available, or
c. Using the **Format**, **Paragraph** menu command.

On the next two pages, we show the text alignment commands using all three methods.

Buttons on Formatting bar	Paragraph Alignment	Keystrokes
	Left	\<Ctrl+L\>
	Centre	\<Ctrl+E\>
	Right	\<Ctrl+R\>
	Justify	\<Ctrl+J\>

Other available shortcut keys for paragraph alignment, are as follows:

To Format	Type
Indent from left margin	Ctrl+M
Decrease indent	Ctrl+Shift+M
Create a hanging indent	Ctrl+T
Decrease a hanging indent	Ctrl+Shift+T
Add or remove 12 points of space before a paragraph	Ctrl+0 (zero)
Remove paragraph formats not applied by a style	Ctrl+Q
Restore default formatting by applying the Normal style	Ctrl+Shift+N
Display or hide non-printing characters (such as · → ¶)	Ctrl+*

The display below shows the dialogue box resulting from using the **Format**, **Paragraph** command.

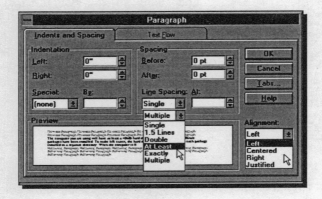

Whichever of the above methods is used, formatting can take place either before or after the text is entered. If formatting is selected first, then text will type in the chosen format until a further formatting command is given. If this method is used, or you choose to operate Word in clear-screen view mode, then the keyboard short cuts will be the fastest method. If, on the other hand, you choose to enter text and then format it afterwards, you must select the text to be formatted (by highlighting it) before you activate a formatting command.

Paragraph Spacing:
A paragraph can be displayed on screen or printed on paper in single-line, 1½-line, or double-line spacing, or you can set the spacing to any value you want with the **At Least** option and then specify what interval you want, as shown on the screen dump above.

The available shortcut keys are as follows:

To Format	*Type*
Single-spaced lines	Ctrl+1
One-and-a-half-spaced lines	Ctrl+5
Double-spaced lines	Ctrl+2

When setting customised alignment indentations you have the choice of 4 units to work with, inches, centimetres, points or picas. These can be selected by using the **Tools**, **Options** command, choosing the **General** tab of the displayed Options dialogue box, and clicking the down arrow against the **Measurement Units** list box, shown open here, which is to be found at the bottom of the dialogue box.

Indenting Text:

Most documents will require some form of paragraph indenting. An indent is the space between the margin and the edge of the text in the paragraph. When an indent is set (on the left or right side of the page), any justification on that side of the page sets at the indent, not the page border.

To illustrate indentation, open the file PCUSERS2, select the first paragraph, and then choose the **Format**, **Paragraph** command. In the **Indentation** field, select 0.5" for both **Left** and **Right**, as shown below. On pressing **OK**, the first selected paragraph is displayed indented.

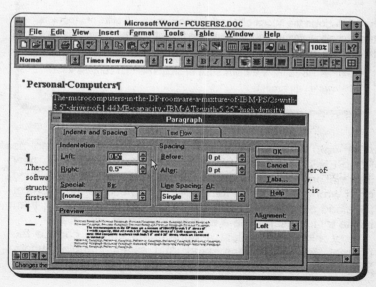

Hanging Indents:

The **Indentation** option of the **Format**, **Paragraph** command, can be used to create 'hanging' indents, where all the lines in a paragraph, including any text on the first line that follows a tab, are indented by a specified amount. This is often used in lists to emphasise certain points.

To illustrate the method, use the PCUSERS1 file and add at the end of it, after the 'C:\>' prompt, the text shown below.

To find out what is on your hard disc, type

DIR   (and press the <Enter> key)

which will produce a list of all the filenames on the 'Root' directory (the one with the C:\> prompt) - directories are displayed with their names in angle brackets, for example <DOS>. If your hard disc is structured correctly, then the programs that make up a package would have been installed in a separate directory. For example:

Name Description

123r4w Holds the LOTUS 1-2-3 Release 4 for Windows spreadsheet package.

QB45 Holds the Microsoft Quick Basic version 4.5 suite of programs which allow you to write and compile fully structured Basic programs. It is one of the best versions of non-visual Basic available on the market.

Windows Holds the Windows suite of programs that controls your Windows environment.

After you have typed it in, save the enlarged memo as PCUSERS3, before going on with formatting the new information. This is done as a precaution in case anything goes wrong with the formatting - it is sometimes much easier to reload a saved file (using the **File**, **Open** command), than it is to try to unscramble a wrongly formatted document!

Now, highlight the last 4 paragraphs above, choose the **Format**, **Paragraph** command, and select 'Hanging' under **Special** and 1" under **By**, as shown on the next page.

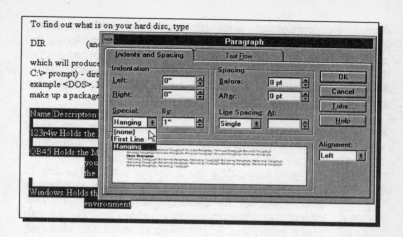

To find out what is on your hard disc, type

DIR   (an[d ...]

which will produce
C:\> prompt) - dire
example <DOS>. I
make up a package

Name Description

123r4w Holds the

QB45 Holds the M
          you
          the

Windows Holds th
          environment

After selecting **OK** the text formats, but it is still highlighted.
To remove the highlighting, click the mouse button on the
page. The second and following lines of the third paragraph
selected, should appear indented 1 inch from the left margin.
This is still not very inspiring, so to complete the effect we will
edit the first lines of each paragraph as follows:

To find out what is on your hard disc, type

DIR   (and press the <Enter> key)

which will produce a list of all the filenames on the 'Root' directory (the one with the
C:\> prompt) - directories are displayed with their names in angle brackets, for
example <DOS>. If your hard disc is structured correctly, then the programs that
make up a package would have been installed in a separate directory. For example:

Name	Description
123r4w	Holds the LOTUS 1-2-3 Release 4 for Windows spreadsheet package.
QB45	Holds the Microsoft Quick Basic version 4.5 suite of programs which allow you to write and compile fully structured Basic programs. It is one of the best versions of non-visual Basic available on the market.
Windows	Holds the Windows suite of programs that controls your Windows environment.

Place the cursor in front of the word 'Description' in paragraph 4 and press the <Tab> key once. This places the start of the word in the same column as the indented text of the third paragraph. To complete the effect place tabs before the word 'Holds' in the next three paragraphs, until your hanging indents are correct.

This may seem like a complicated rigmarole to go through each time you want the hanging indent effect, but with Word you will eventually set up all your indents, etc., in templates. Then all you do is click in a paragraph to produce them.

When you finish formatting the document, save it under its current filename with either the **File, Save** command (<Ctrl+S>), or by clicking the Save button. This command does not display a dialogue box, so you use it when you do not need to make any changes to the saving operation.

Inserting Bullets:

Bullets are small characters you can insert, anywhere you like, in the text of your document to improve visual impact In Word there are several choices for displaying lists with bullets or numbers. These are made available through the **Format**, **Bullets and Numbering** command, which displays the following dialogue box:

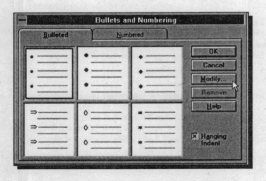

You can select any of the bullets shown here, or you could click the **Modify** button to change the size of the bullet or the indentation.

Further, by pressing the **Bullet** button on the Modify Bulleted List dialogue box which would be displayed, you could select any character from the Symbol typeface or other available type-faces.

74

If you select the **Numbered** tab, a similar dialogue box is displayed, giving you a choice of several numbering systems and the ability to modify them.

Once inserted, you can copy, move or cut a bulleted line in the same way as any other text. However, you can not use the <BkSp> or <Del> keys to delete a bullet.

Inserting Date and Time:

You can insert today's date, the date the current document was created or was last revised, or a date or time that reflects the current system date and time into a document. Therefore, the date can be a date that changes, or a date that always stays the same. In either case, the date is inserted in a date field.

To insert a date field in your document, place the cursor where you want to insert the date, select the **Insert**, **Date and Time** command and choose one of the displayed date formats which suits you from the dialogue box shown below.

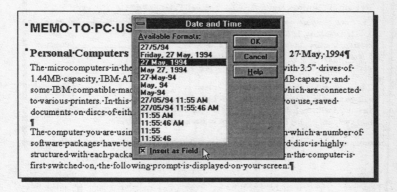

Highlighting '27 May, 1994' (or whatever date is current), checking the the **Insert as field box,** and pressing **OK**, inserts the date in our document at the chosen position. The above screen is a composite of the operation required and the result of that operation.

If you save a document with a date field in it and you open it a few days later, the date shown on it will be the original date the document was created. Should you want to update this date to the current date, right-click the field and select the **Update Field** option from the displayed Quick menu.

Word can either display the codes kept in a field, such as a date field, or the field results. To toggle between these two displays, place the insertion pointer anywhere within a field, click the right mouse button to display the Quick menu, shown below, and select the **Toggle Field Codes** option. The date field then changes to:

{TIME \@ "d MMMM, yyyy"}

as shown below.

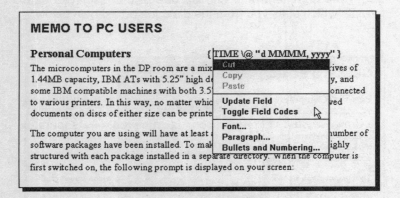

The reason for this facility is that you might want to mix two different types of formats, so the opportunity is presented for you to edit the code within a field.

In the screen dump above, we have removed the various display markers by pressing the Show/Hide button on the Toolbar.

Inserting Annotations:

Another powerful feature of Word is the facility to annotate a document. These act like electronic labels - initialled comments by the people who might have an input to a document, as shown below.

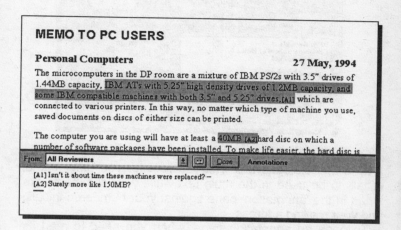

Each person who views and edits the same document is identified as **A1**, **A2**, etc., which are used to mark the place in the text where an annotation is required. A separate annotation pane holds the actual comments.

To add annotations to a document, place the cursor at the place you want to add a comment (or highlight a portion of text), and use the **Insert**, **Annotation** command.

If you want the program to use your initials, instead of A1, etc., use the **Tools, Options** command and click on the **User Info** tab on the Options dialogue box which displays what is shown on the next page.

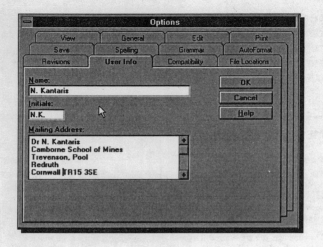

It is in this dialogue box that you register your user name, initials to be used in the main text while your comments are typed in the 'annotation' pane against your numbered initials, and your mailing address.

To open an annotation pane, when you need to read its contents, double-click on the numbered initials in the text with the mouse pointer. To remove an annotation, highlight the initials in the text and press <Del>.

7. PAGE LAYOUT IN WORD

Page layout is a combination of page set-up, the paragraph styles and formats of the text and graphics on that page.

Page Format in Word

You can format a page in Word by using the **Format** command from the menu bar, then selecting in turn the various options displayed here in the pull-down sub-menu, from **Paragraph** to **Style**. In addition, a page can be set up by selecting the **File, Page Setup** command (to be discussed in detail shortly).

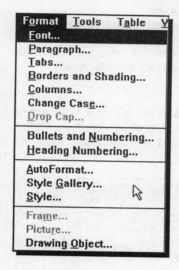

The settings specified in both the **Page Setup** and in most of the **Format** sub-menu options, can be applied to the whole document, from the current cursor position for the rest of the document, or just for selected text. Page layout can also be included in the template that you select when you create a document, with the **File**, **New** command, since it includes paragraph styles which in turn specify page settings.

A page layout includes settings for the following:

- Top, bottom, left, right, and gutter margins
- Page size and orientation
- Number of columns, and space between each column
- Left, centre, right, decimal, and leader tab stops
- Placement of headers and/or footers
- Section layout commands which control the starting point for the section text, line numbering, vertical alignment of text, and display of footnotes
- Placement and style of lines around page and between columns.

Page Set-up

You can modify your page set-up from any Word view. However, you can only see the changes you make take effect correctly, if you are in Page Layout mode, or you select the **File, Print Preview** command.

To illustrate page set-ups, first **Open** the PCUSERS3 document, and then use the **File, Page Setup** command to display the Page Setup dialogue box. Note that at the top of the dialogue box there are four tabs which select the type of page attribute you would like to change.

When the page set-up is altered, Word reformats the document using that set-up. Any changes you make are effective only for the current document, unless you save the page set-up to the existing (or a new) style, or template.

Modifying Margins:

You can change the standard page margins for your entire document, from the cursor position onward, or if you have selected some text prior to opening the 'Page Setup' box, for the selected text.

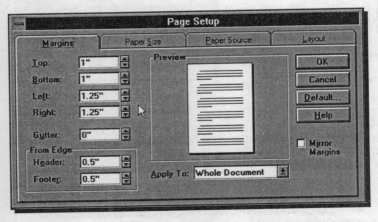

This dialogue box is obtained initially when the **Page Setup** command is selected, or when the **Margins** option tab is clicked. It lets you control your paper margins (the blank areas around the edges). The 'Preview' page in the middle of the box shows how your changes will look on a real page.

Modifying Paper Size:

Selecting the next option tab, **Paper Size**, in the above dialogue box, allows you to select the paper size relevant to your printer. In our case, the displayed paper size is A4 (see below), since we changed it earlier. Clicking on the down-arrow of the paper size box reveals the available paper and envelope sizes.

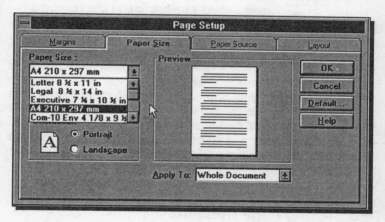

Check that the paper size matches that in your printer, otherwise you may get strange results. The orientation of the printed page is normally **Portrait** (text prints across the page width), but you could choose to change this to **Landscape** which prints across the page length, as long as your printer can print in landscape.

Modifying Paper Source:

Clicking on the third 'Page Setup' tab, displays yet another dialogue box, part of which is shown here, from which you can select the paper source. You might have a printer that holds paper in trays, in which case you might want to specify that the first page (headed paper perhaps), should be taken from one tray, while the rest of the paper should be taken from a different tray.

Modifying the Page Layout:

Clicking the last 'Page Setup' tab displays the Layout dialogue box, part of which is shown here. From this dialogue box you can set options for headers and footers, section breaks, vertical alignment and whether to add line numbers.

The default for **Section Start** is 'New Page' which allows the section to start at the top of the next page. Pressing the down-arrow against this option allows you to change this choice. In the Headers and Footers box you can specify whether you want one header or footer for even-numbered pages and a different header or footer for odd-numbered pages. You can further specify if you want a different header or footer on the first page from the header or footer used for the rest of the document. Word can align the top line with the 'Top' margin, but this can be changed with the **Vertical Alignment** option.

Formatting Page Columns

You can quickly modify the number of displayed columns, either for the whole document or for selected text by using the Columns button from the Toolbar, shown here. However, if you want more control over how the columns are displayed, then use the **Format, Columns** command. On the facing page, we have selected the second paragraph of the PCUSERS3 memo and then used the **Format, Columns** command to format it in two columns with 0.5" in between the two columns.

To see how the 'Preview' page changes, click the appropriate button on the **Presets** field of the Columns dialogue box. Now change the **Space Between** (otherwise known as gutter width) to see how to set the separation zones between columns.

If you want to be able to see the result of your selection on your actual text, use the **View** command and select the **Page Layout** mode. As usual, you will only see your selected text in two columns, after you press the **OK** button on the Columns dialogue box.

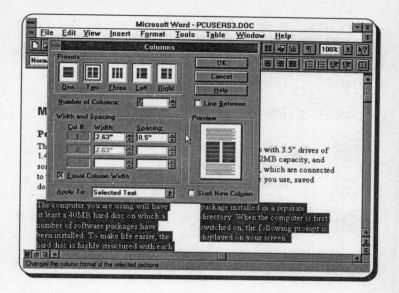

Formatting Page Tabs

You can format text in columns by using tab stops. Word has default left tab stops every 0.5 inch from the left margin, as shown here. This symbol appears on the left edge of the ruler (see below).

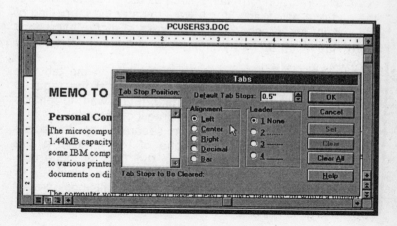

To set tabs, use either the **Format**, **Tabs** command which produces the Tab dialogue box, or click on the tab symbol on the left of the Ruler which rotates through the available tab stops.

The tab stop types available have the following function:

Button	Name	Effect
	Left	Left aligns text after the tab stop.
	Centre	Centres text on tab stop.
	Right	Right aligns text after the tab stop.
	Decimal	Aligns decimal point with tab stop.

To clear the ruler of tab settings press the **Clear All** button on the Tabs dialogue box. When you set a tab stop on the ruler, all default tab stops to the left of the one you are setting are removed. In addition, tab stops apply either to the paragraph containing the cursor, or to any selected paragraphs.

As all paragraph formatting, such as tab stops, is placed at the end of a paragraph, if you want to carry the formatting of the current paragraph to the next, press <Enter>. If you don't want formatting to carry on, press the down arrow key instead.

The easiest way to set a tab is to click on the tab type button you want and then point and click at the required position on the lower half of the ruler. If you want to remove an added tab, point to it, click and drag it off the ruler.

If you want tabular text to be separated by characters instead of by spaces, select one of the three available characters from the **Leader** box in the Tabs dialogue box. The options are none (the default), dotted, dashed, or underline. The Contents and Index pages of this book are set with right tabs and dotted leader characters.

Formatting with Styles

We saw earlier in Chapter 6, how you can format your work using Paragraph Styles, but we confined ourselves to using the default **Normal** style only. In this section we will get to grips with how to create, modify, use, and manage styles.

As mentioned previously, a Paragraph Style is a set of formatting instructions which you save so that you can use repeatedly within a document or in different documents. A collection of Paragraph Styles forms a Style Sheet which could be deemed appropriate for, say, all your memos, so it can be used to preserve uniformity. It maintains consistency and saves time by not having to format each paragraph individually. Further, should you decide to change a style, all the paragraphs associated with that style reformat automatically. Finally, if you want to provide a pattern for shaping a final document, then you use what is known as a Template. All documents which have not been assigned a document template, use the **Normal.dot** template, by default.

Paragraph Styles:

Paragraph Styles contain paragraph and character formats and a name can be attached to these formatting instructions. From then on, applying the style name is the same as formatting that paragraph with the same instructions.

You can create a style by example, either with the use of the Formatting Toolbar or the keyboard, or you can create a style from scratch, before you use it, by selecting the **Format, Style** menu command. By far the simplest way of creating a style is by example from the Formatting Toolbar.

Creating Paragraph Styles by Example:

In a previous chapter we spent some time manually creating some hanging indents in the last few paragraphs of the PCUSERS4 document. To create a style from this previous work, place the insertion pointer in one of these paragraphs, say, in the 'Name Description' line, and highlight the entire name of the existing style in the Formatting Toolbar's Style box, as shown on the next page.

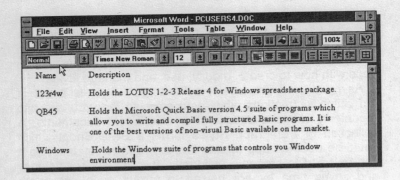

Then, type the new style name you want to create, say, 'Hanging Indent', and press <Enter>.

Finally, highlight the last three paragraphs with hanging indents and change their style to the new 'Hanging Indent', by clicking the mouse in the Style box button and selecting the appropriate style from the displayed list, as shown below.

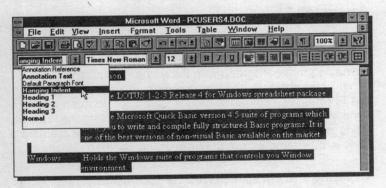

Creating Styles with the Menu Command:

You can create, or change, a style before you apply any formatting to a paragraph, by using the **Format**, **Style** command, which displays the dialogue box shown on the next page.

From here you can choose which style you want to change by selecting a style from the displayed **Styles** list. If you are not changing an existing style, skip the above procedure.

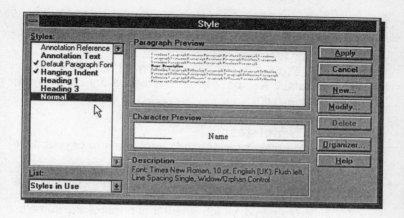

In either case, press the **Modify** button which produces the following dialogue box:

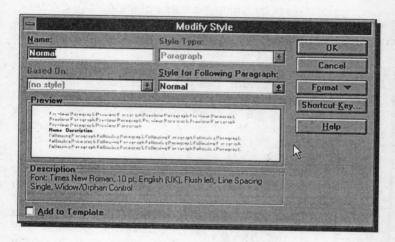

From here you can create a new style, or modify an existing style, by changing the formatting of characters, borders, paragraphs, and tab stops. You can even select which style should follow your current style.

If you have a lot of changes to make to a style, or you are creating your own personal style sheet, then it might be better if you created a template and defined your styles within it.

From then on, each time you want to use your special styles, simply begin with your customised template rather than the default **Normal** template.

Note that Word has a default **Normal** template which contains a default **Normal** style sheet with a default **Normal** paragraph style in it!

Document Templates:

A document template provides the overall pattern of your final document. It can contain:

- Paragraph styles and style sheets, which can control your paragraph and page set-up.
- Boilerplate text, which is text that remains the same in every document.
- AutoText (Glossary in previous versions), which is standard text and graphics that you could insert in a document by typing the name of the AutoText entry.
- Macros, which are programs that can change the menus and key assignments to comply with the type of document you are creating.

As we have said before, every document has a template. If you don't assign a template to a document, then the default **Normal.dot** template is used by Word. To create a new document template, you either modify an existing one, create one from scratch, or create one based on the formatting of an existing document.

To illustrate this last point, we will create a simple document template, which we will call **Pcuser**, based on the formatting of the PCUSERS4 document. But first, make sure you have defined the 'Hanging Indent' style as explained earlier, and that the file is opened. Then select the **File, New** command which displays the New dialogue box, shown here.

From this dialogue box you can create a new document or a new template. Select **Template** in the **New** field box, type in the **Template** box the name of the document (and its extension) on which you want the new template to be based, fill in the **Summary** information, and press **OK**.

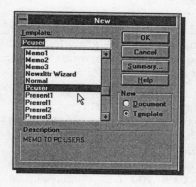

Next, choose the **File, Save As** command, type the template name (**Pcuser** in this case), and press the **OK** button.

To use the new template, use the **File, New** command which causes the New dialogue box to be displayed. Select the name of the Template you want to use, from the **Template** list, and press the **OK** button.

Templates can also contain Macros as well as AutoText; macros allow you to automate Word keystroke actions only, while AutoText speeds up the addition of boilerplate text and graphics into your document. Macros and AutoText will be discussed in more detail later in a separate chapter.

To specify the location of a macro or AutoText entry into

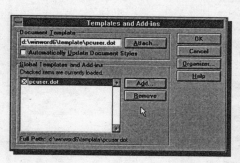

your document, use the **File, Templates** command to display the Templates and Add-Ins dialogue box shown here.

To make a macro and/or an AutoText entry available to all documents, press the **Add** button and select **Pcuser.dot**

from the displayed list. To make the macro and/or AutoText entry only available to documents based on the current template, uncheck the square to the left of the template name.

Storing macros and/or AutoText entries as global, makes them available to all your documents. However, doing this with a large number of these can clutter your **Normal.dot** file. That is why macros designed to do a specific job should be kept with the appropriate template.

Special Formatting Features
Word has several special formatting features which force text to override style and style sheet formatting. In what follows, we discuss the most important amongst these.

Changing the Default Character Format:
As we have seen, Word uses the Times New Roman type font with a 10 points size as the default for the **Normal** style, which is contained in the **Normal** template, for all new documents. If the majority of your work demands some different font style or size, then you can change these defaults to suit youself.

To change the default character formatting, use the **Format**, **Font** command, select the new defaults you want to use, and press the **Default** button, as shown below:

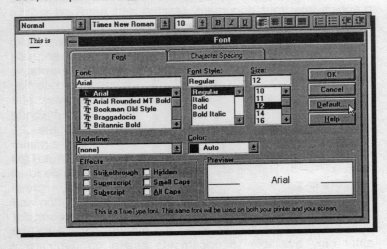

On pressing the **Default** button, the following dialogue box is displayed:

Pressing the **Yes** button, changes the default character settings for this and all subsequent new documents, but does not change already existing ones.

Inserting Special Characters and Symbols:

Word has a collection of Symbol fonts, such as the characters produced by the Symbol, Wingdings and Zapf Dingbats character sets, from which you can select characters and insert them into your document using the **Insert, Symbol** command.

When this command is executed, Word displays the following dialogue box:

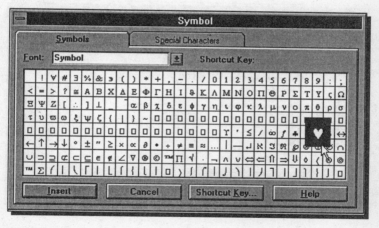

Pressing the down-arrow button next to the **Font** box, reveals the other available character sets. The set showing above is the Symbol set. If you point and click the left mouse button at a character within the set, it selects it. If you press down the left mouse button it magnifies the selected character, and if you double-click the left mouse button, it transfers the selected character to your document at the insertion point. A Symbol character can only be deleted with the <Del> key; you can not use the <BkSp> key to delete it.

91

The advantage of using Symbol is that Word embeds codes in your document which prevent you from changing the character by selecting it and changing to a different font. Thus, this type of formatting overrides any changes you might introduce with a new paragraph formatting.

Inserting Other Special Characters:

You can include other special characters in a document, such as optional hyphens, which remain invisible until they are needed to hyphenate a word at the end of a line; non-breaking hyphens, which prevent unwanted hyphenation; non-breaking spaces, which prevent two words from splitting at the end of a line; or opening and closing single quotes. To insert these characters, click at the **Special Characters** tab of the Symbol dialogue box which reveals the following:

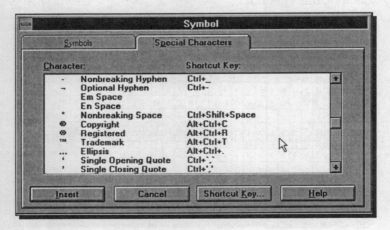

To insert one of these special characters, simply highlight the one required and press the **Insert** button. Using the **Shortcut Key** button displays the shortcut key combination attached to a symbol or special character, if it exists. You can also use this option to attach your preferred shortcut key combination to a symbol or special character.

8. FRAMES AND DRAWINGS

A frame in Word is like a 'mini-document' within the main document that allows you to create multiple layouts on the same page. A frame can contain text, a drawing, a picture, or an object such as a Lotus 1-2-3 worksheet, an AmiPro document, or a Word equation. A frame is not affected by the formatting of the main document. You can make document text wrap around, or flow above and below a frame; using the latter, you can create a heading to span a multi-column page. A page can contain multiple frames which can overlap.

Creating Frames

With Word you can create an empty frame by using the **Insert, Frame** command. You must, however, make sure that you are in Page Layout mode first. If you are not, the program will warn you and switch you to the required view.

Selecting this command, opens a cross-hair on your display and by moving this to the desired position, then pressing the left mouse button and dragging the mouse, you can insert a frame of the required size in your document, as shown below:

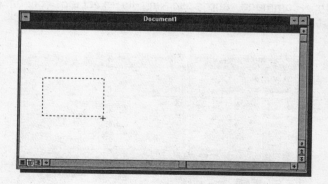

When you create a frame, it is placed in your document with the insertion point blinking in the upper left corner within the frame. When you type text, it wraps to fit the frame, but the frame expands vertically to accommodate all the typed text.

Moving Frames

A frame can be moved around your document by first selecting it, then dragging it with the mouse (move the mouse pointer over the frame until it turns to a four-headed arrow, as shown below in the top-left position, then click and drag to the desired position). The dotted outline shows the position in which the frame will be placed once you let go the left mouse button.

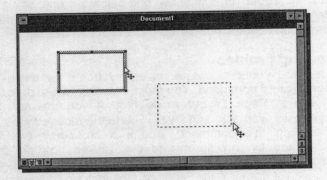

Another way of moving a frame is by using the **Format, Frame** command, and specifying its exact position on the page in the Frame box shown below.

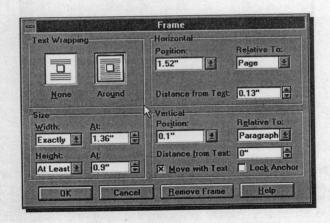

If a frame is placed in the middle of an existing paragraph, the text of that paragraph can either wrap around the frame, as shown below, or be split above and below the frame. This depends on the selected **Text Wrapping** option in the Frame dialogue box, with **Around** being the default.

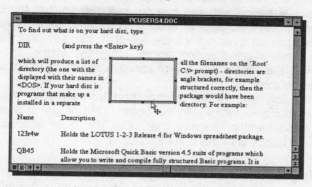

Also by default, framed objects move with their surrounding text. To fix a frame at a specific position on a page, use the **Format, Frame** command and de-select the **Move with Text** option.

Word allows you to select a paragraph, a table or a drawing and then frame it, as shown below:

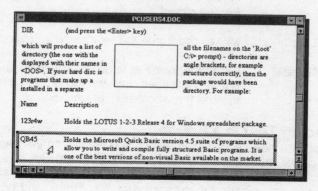

Once an object is framed, it can be moved in exactly the same way as an empty frame by dragging the dotted frame with the mouse pointer.

Sizing Frames

There are two ways of sizing frames; with the mouse or the keyboard using the Frame dialogue box.

Sizing a Frame with the Mouse:

To size a frame with the mouse, select it so that the black selection handles appear around the frame, then move the mouse pointer over one of the selection handles until it turns to the two-headed sizing arrow. Drag the sizing arrow to change the frame to the required size, then release the mouse button.

Dragging one of the corner handles will drag the two attached frame sides with the pointer, but dragging a centre line handle will only move that side. Try these actions until you are happy with the resultant frame.

Sizing a Frame with the Keyboard:

To size a frame with the keyboard, first select the frame, then use the **Format, Frame** command which displays the Frame dialogue box. In this box, select the **Width** and **Height** options.

The **Width** and **Height** options have the following effect:

Auto   Gives the frame the same size as the
            framed object.

Exactly   Makes the frame the exact size you specify.

At Least   Gives the frame at least the specified height,
            but it increases the height to be able to
            include the whole text, or graphic.

Placing Text in a Frame

Once you have your frame where you want it on the page, it is only of any use if you do something with it. So, click the mouse pointer inside the frame, which displays the sizing handles and places the cursor inside the frame, and type in some text (see screen display on next page). In our example, we also chose to name the style within the frame as 'framed' using the **Format, Style** command.

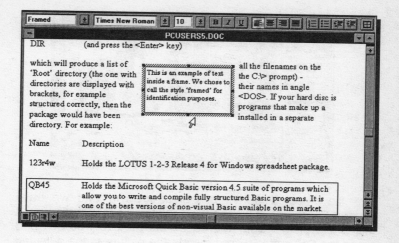

Next, and while the cursor is within the frame, select 'hanging indent' as the new style for the text inside your frame. The frame disappears, but the text remains as a redefined paragraph. If you choose the 'framed' style, the frame will reappear with the text intact inside it.

Now save this as PCUSERS5, then click the mouse button outside the frame. This will cancel the frame selection and you will not be able to access, or edit, the text inside the frame until you next click inside it. Moving the mouse pointer over the frame area, turns it into a four-headed arrow, allowing you to move the frame to a new position when you click and drag. You can select the frame by single clicking which will let you re-size it; clicking once more anywhere on the text within the frame, allows you to edit that text.

Importing a Picture into a Frame

Create another frame on your page and click inside to select it. To import a picture into this frame, select the **Insert, Picture** command, which will open the dialogue box shown on the next page.

This box allows you to enter the details of the picture, or graphic, that you want to import. The **List Files of Type** box gives you the choice of a wide range of graphic formats, but we will use a graphics sample from the **clipart** subdirectory.

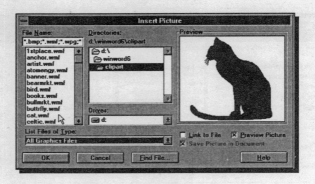

The file selected above is called **cat.wmf** and we have chosen to preview it by checking the **Preview Picture** box. If this is the picture you like, check the **Link to File** box and press the **OK** button. Word inserts the picture in the selected frame, as shown below:

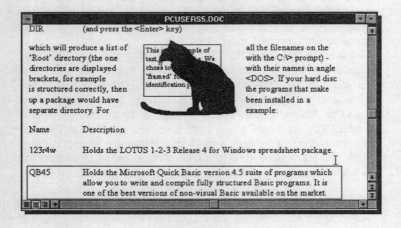

Save the resultant document as PCUSERS6.

You can change the scaling factor of a picture and size it either by using the mouse, or by using the **Format**, **Picture** command. The latter method causes the Picture dialogue box to be displayed, as shown on the next page.

If you want more white space around a picture, use negative numbers in the **Crop From** fields.

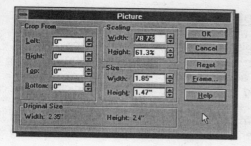

A picture can be inserted directly into your document at the cursor position, or you can first insert a frame, then insert the picture into the frame.

The advantage of the latter is that your text can be made to wrap around a frame, so you have more control over the inserted picture.

You can add a variety of borders to a frame, or a picture, by using the **F̲ormat**, **B̲orders and Shading** command which displays the following dialogue box:

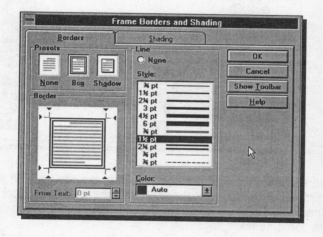

From here, you can select the thickness of the border line, whether it will have a single or double-line border, and whether the border should have a shadow or not. You can also choose the type of shading you prefer within the border area, by pressing the **S̲hading** tab.

The Drawing Tool

As long as you have a mouse, you can use Word's Draw tool to create, or edit, a picture consisting of lines, arcs, ellipses, rectangles, and even text boxes. These can either exist in their own right, or be additions to a picture.

If you want to add a drawing to an existing picture, first select it, then use the **Edit, Picture Object** command. Activating this command while the picture of the cat in PCUSERS6 document is selected, produces the following display:

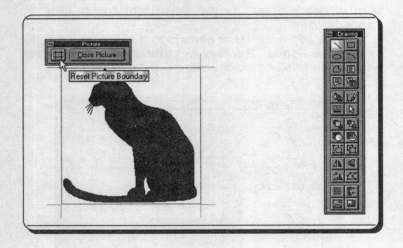

The Draw tool can also be activated by double-clicking within a picture. You cannot, though, activate the Draw tool with either of the above methods if you are dealing with a frame that contains text.

To add a drawing to any frame or to any other part of your document, click at the Draw button on the Standard Toolbar, shown here. To actually draw within a frame you must first select it before starting to draw.

Whichever way you activate the Draw tool, Word displays a new set of icons on the right side of your document as shown above. These can be moved to form a third Toolbar.

The Drawing icons allow you to carry out the following tasks:

Draw a line	Draw a rectangle
Draw an ellipse	Draw an arc
Draw in freehand	Text Box
Callout	Format Callout
Fill Colour	Line Colour
Line Style	Select Draw Objects
Bring to Front	Send to Back
Bring to Front of Text	Send Behind Text
Group	Ungroup
Flip Horizontal	Flip Vertical
Rotate Right	Reshape
Snap to Grid	Align Drawing Objects
Create Picture	Insert Frame

The effects of these drawing tools can be superimposed on either the document area or within a frame which might contain a picture. The result is that you can annotate drawings and pictures to your total satisfaction.

Creating a Drawing

To create an object, click on the required Draw button, such as the ellipse or rectangle, position the mouse pointer where you want to create the object on the screen, and then drag the mouse to draw the object. Hold the <Shift> key while you drag the mouse to create a perfect circle or square. If you do not hold <Shift>, Word creates an ellipse or a rectangle.

You can use the Freehand/Polygon Draw button to create freehand objects. First click on the Freehand button, then position the mouse pointer where you want to create the object on the screen. If you then press the left mouse button and keep it pressed, you can draw freehand. If, on the other hand, you click the left mouse button, the edge of the line attaches itself on the drawing area, at the point of contact. A straight line can then be drawn between that point and the next point on which you happen to click the mouse button. In this way you can draw polygons. When you finish drawing with either of these two methods, either double-click or press the <Esc> key to finish.

Editing a Drawing:

To select an object, first click the 'Selection Arrow' button and then click the desired object. Word displays black handles around the object selected.

You can move an object, or multiple objects, within a draw area by selecting them and dragging to the desired position. To copy an object, click at the object, then use the **Edit, Copy / Edit, Paste** commands.

To size an object, position the mouse pointer on a black handle and then drag the handle until the object is the desired shape and size.

To delete an object, select the object and press <Del>. To delete a drawing, hold the <Shift> key down and click each object in turn that makes up the drawing, unless they are grouped or framed, then press <Del>.

Do try out some of these commands using the PCUSERS6 document file. You could experiment with different text fonts, and try to edit the cat picture. As long as you do not save the results of your experimentation under the same file name, you can try different variations to the layout without fear of losing the contents of the original file.

Using Layered Drawings:

You can use Draw's Bring to Front or Send to Back buttons to determine the order of layered drawings. Drawings, or pictures, layered on top of each other can create useful visual effects, provided you remember that the top drawing and/or picture obscures the one below it, as shown below.

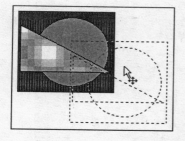

Here we have used Draw's Rectangle, Ellipse, and Freehand buttons to draw the three displayed shapes. The order you draw these is not important as you can use the Bring to Front and Send to Back buttons to rearrange them to your taste. We then selected each shape in turn, and used the Fill Colour button to give them different shades. Finally, we selected each shape, while holding down the <Shift> key, then used the Group button to lock them together, before attempting to move the whole group down and to the right (you can tell they are grouped because attempting to move them, moves the whole group, shown above in a dotted outline).

Changing Draw's Defaults

You can change the **F**ill colour palette, **L**ine thickness, colour and arrowhead style, and **Si**z**e and Position** of your drawing

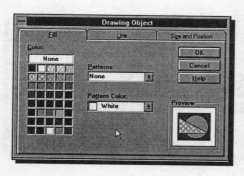

by using the **Format, Drawing Object** command, which displays the Drawing Object dialogue box shown here. You can even preview proposed changes to the selected drawing before accepting them.

Inserting Objects into a Document

You can insert an Object into a document by using the **Insert, Object** command which causes the following dialogue box to appear on your screen:

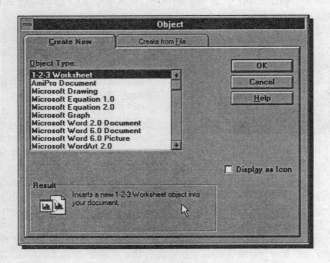

From here, you can choose different 'Object Types', from Lotus 1-2-3 Worksheets to Word Documents. For example, if you select 'Microsoft Equation 2' from the **Object Type** list, Word displays the equation editor shown below. This allows you to build mathematical equations which can then be included in your Word for Windows document.

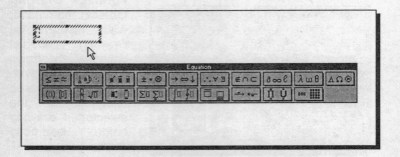

If, on the other hand, you select Microsoft Graph, or you press the Graph button on Word's Standard Toolbar, shown here, and you don't have a table in your document, the following screen is displayed:

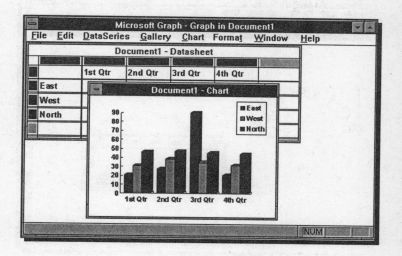

This is an internal Word example, showing the capabilities of the package. If you did have a table within your document which included information that could be graphed (see next chapter), and you had selected the area of the table you wanted to display as a graph, then Word would have displayed the contents of the selected portion of your table in an appropriate chart-type graph.

Finally, selecting Microsoft WordArt 2, causes the display on the next page to appear on your screen. If Word informs you that it cannot find the Microsoft WordArt file, make sure that the PATH in your **autoexec.bat** file contains the entry C:\Windows\Msapps\Wordart, even if you have elected to install Word on another drive; Word installs Wordart on the C: drive.

We have typed in the text area of the dialogue box the entry 'PC User Club', then selected the 'Arch Up' Style from the first list which normally displays 'Straight Line'.

You can choose from a selection of different fonts, size, and styles which can then be aligned in different areas of your document.

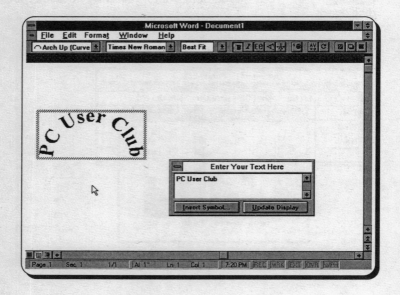

Closing the dialogue box, leaves your artwork at the original cursor position within your document. From there, it can be repositioned within the current document, or placed on the clipboard for transfer to a different document. We have transferred the above entry to the top of the PCUSERS6 document and then saved the result as PCUSERS7.

9. MORE ADVANCED TECHNIQUES

Microsoft has built many advanced features into Word. Amongst these, we will examine here what you are most likely to need and in the order we assume you will require them. We shall examine document spell and grammar checking, the use of the thesaurus, page numbering, inclusion of headers/footers and footnotes.

Document Checking

When you have entered all the text and graphics into your document and selected suitable formats, there is only the process of correcting your work before printing the final copy. Word has many built-in tools to speed this process up and we will briefly describe the main ones here. There is also a set of Toolbar buttons for document checking and correcting.

Using the Spell Checker:

Most people have trouble spelling at least some words, but with Word that is not a problem. The package has a very comprehensive spell checker and has the ability to add specialised and personal dictionaries. The main dictionary contains more that 100,000 words which cannot be edited. The user dictionary you can customise and edit. If you are using personal dictionaries (see next page) and you use the spell checker and choose **Add**, Word adds the word to the specified user dictionary, which should have the file extension .dic.

 To spell check your document, either click the 'Spelling' button on the Standard Toolbar, shown here, or use the **Tools**, **Spelling** command (or **F7**) to open the dialogue box shown on the next page.

Word starts spell checking from the point of insertion onwards. If you want to check a word or paragraph only, highlight it first. If you want to spell check the whole document, move the insertion point to the beginning of the document before starting. Once Word has found a misspelled word, you can correct it in the **Change To** box, or select a word from the **Suggestions** list.

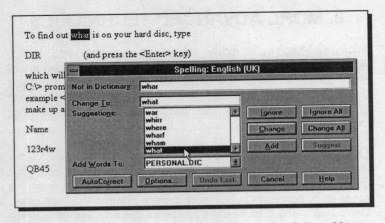

To find out **whar** is on your hard disc, type

DIR   (and press the <Enter> key)

which will
C:\> prom
example <
make up a

Name

123r4w

QB45

Spelling: English (UK)

Not in Dictionary: whar

Change To: what

Suggestions:
war
whirr
where
wharf
wham
what

Add Words To: PERSONAL.DIC

AutoCorrect   Options...   Undo Last   Cancel   Help

Ignore   Ignore All
Change   Change All
Add   Suggest

Word will produce a suggestions list only if the **Always Suggest** option from the Options dialogue box, shown below, is checked. This dialogue box is displayed if you press the **Options** button from the opening dialogue box.

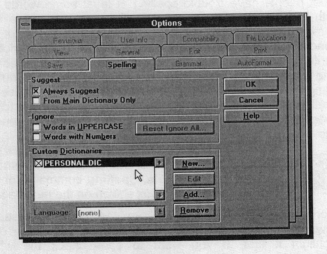

Options

Revisions   User Info   Compatibility   File Locations
View   General   Edit   Print
Save   Spelling   Grammar   AutoFormat

Suggest
[X] Always Suggest
[ ] From Main Dictionary Only

Ignore
[ ] Words in UPPERCASE   Reset Ignore All...
[ ] Words with Numbers

Custom Dictionaries
[X] PERSONAL.DIC

New...
Edit
Add...
Remove

Language: [none]

OK
Cancel
Help

To use a personal dictionary, uncheck the **From Main Dictionary Only** box, click the **New** button and give your dictionary a name. On return to the spell checking operation, the **Add** button on the Spelling dialogue box is not dimmed anymore and, therefore, can be used.

In the Options dialogue box you can select **Words in UPPERCASE** which will cause the spell checker to ignore words in all uppercase letters, and/or you can select **Words with Numbers** which forces the spell checker to ignore all words that include numbers.

When the correct word appears in the **Change To** box (you could choose a different word from the **Suggestions** list), select the **Change** button to replace the misspelled word in your document with the selected word. You select the **Change** button to correct only the current error, otherwise use the **Change All** button to change every future occurrence of the incorrect word in the document.

If you don't want to change the word in your document, use the **Ignore** button to leave that word as is, or the **Ignore All** button to ignore all future occurrences of the word in the document. If, on the other hand, Word comes across a specialised word that it thinks is misspelled, but it is not, you can add it to the customised dictionary named in the **Add Words To** box. This customised dictionary is kept in the **Windows\Msapps\Proof** directory and can be opened like any other file, so that you can edit it. Words are kept in it in alphabetical order.

If you create a custom dictionary in a language other than English, select the **Language** in the Options dialogue box before pressing the **OK** button. To install the language dictionary, use the **Tools, Language** command to mark the text and identify the language it is written in, otherwise, Word will assume that the whole document is written in English. When this is done, Word will use the custom dictionary in the identified language to check text formatted in that language.

You can use the AutoCorrect feature to correct the spelling of words as you type. When this feature is activated and you make a mistake as you type, AutoCorrect replaces it with the correct word. This feature can also be used to replace straight quotation marks with curly ones. To correct typing errors automatically, use the **Tools, AutoCorrect** command and select the **Replace Text as You Type** option in the displayed dialogue box, shown on the next page.

To add an AutoCorrect word while spell checking, click the **AutoCorrect** button in the Spelling dialogue box.

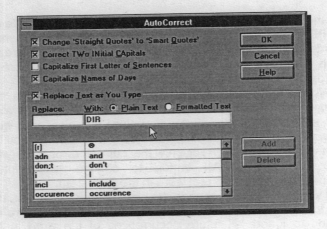

When Word finds double words, for example, yes yes, the **Not in Dictionary** box changes to the **Repeated Word** box with the repeated word displayed, and the **Change** button becomes a **Delete** button. If you want to delete one of the repeated words, leave the **Change To** box blank, and press the **Delete** button.

Using the Thesaurus:

If you are not sure of the meaning of a word, or you want to use an alternative word in your document, then the thesaurus is an indispensable tool. To use the thesaurus, simply place the cursor on the word you want to look up and select **Tools, Thesaurus** (or <Shift+F7>). As long as the word is recognised the following box will open.

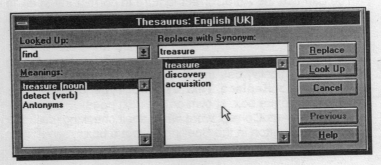

This is a very powerful tool. You can see information about an item in the **Meanings** list, or you can look up a synonym in the **Synonym** list. To change the word in the **Replace with Synonym** text box, select an offered word in either the **Meanings** or **Synonym** list box, or type a word directly into the text box.

You can use the thesaurus like a simple dictionary by typing any word into the **Replace with Synonym** box and selecting **Look Up**. If the word is recognised, lists of its meaning variations and synonyms will be displayed. Pressing the **Replace** button will place the word into the document.

The Grammar Checker:

The grammar checker provided with Word 6 for Windows, is much more flexible than that provided with previous versions of the program, and indeed with other word processors. The idea is excellent, but you must first customise the grammar checker to your requirements.

In order to illustrate what happens when using the grammar checker, open the PCUSERS7 file and select the **Tools**, **Grammar** command. The grammar checker begins by highlighting the first sentence of the memo, then reverts to the spell checker, and eventually returns to the screen shown below.

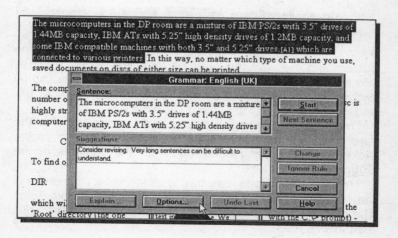

With Word's grammar checker, you have the choice of three pre-set types of writing styles, namely 'Strictly (All Rules)', 'For Business Writing', and 'For Casual Writing'. You also have the choice of three Custom styles. One of these can be selected by pressing the **Options** button of the Grammar dialogue box which displays the dialogue box below. Further, each of the selected styles can be customised by pressing the **Customize Settings** button which displays an additional dialogue box, also shown below.

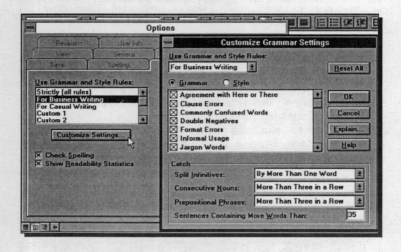

As you can see, you will need to spend quite some time customising the way the grammar checker works. Perhaps you might choose to stop it from re-checking your spelling by clicking at the **Check Spelling** box to be found at the bottom-left corner of the Options dialogue box.

The dialogue box shown on the next page appears on the screen when the last sentence of the paragraph above the dialogue box is being analysed. Note the contents of the **Suggestions** text box.

This same message was also given for every sentence in the document prior to the one being analysed at this point. The message reads 'This main clause may contain a verb in the passive voice'.

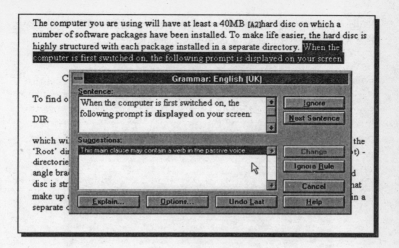

The computer you are using will have at least a 40MB [A2]hard disc on which a number of software packages have been installed. To make life easier, the hard disc is highly structured with each package installed in a separate directory. When the computer is first switched on, the following prompt is displayed on your screen

Grammar: English (UK)

Sentence:
When the computer is first switched on, the following prompt is displayed on your screen:

Suggestions:
This main clause may contain a verb in the passive voice

Ignore
Next Sentence
Change
Ignore Rule
Cancel

Explain... | Options... | Undo Last | Help

On pressing the **Explain** button, the Grammar Explanation box, shown below, is displayed.

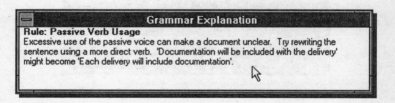

Grammar Explanation

Rule: Passive Verb Usage
Excessive use of the passive voice can make a document unclear. Try rewriting the sentence using a more direct verb. 'Documentation will be included with the delivery' might become 'Each delivery will include documentation'.

The analysis carried out previously was made with the **For Business Writing** option selected, which perhaps explains the comments of the grammar checker. When the option was changed to **For Casual Writing**, the same suggestions were made regarding the 'passive voice' with the same explanations.

In Word 6 for Windows you can stop the grammar checker alerting you with reference to passive verbs, by simply de-selecting the option from the **Grammar** list box of the Customize Grammar Settings dialogue box - a facility not available previously.

If you persevere to the end of the document, Word displays
the following Readability Statistics dialogue box:

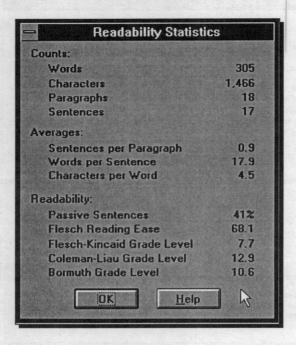

This gives a wealth of information, including readability
measurements, under such terms as Flesch Reading Ease
and Flesch-Kincaid Grade Level, both based on the average
number of syllables per word and average number of words
per sentence (the first giving scores between 0-100 with
standard writing range from 60 to 70, while the second giving
the grade-school level of understanding with standard writing
scoring between 7 and 8).

The last two categories under the readability section
measure word length in characters and sentence length in
words to determine a grade level.

Document Enhancements

In this section we discuss features that enhance a document's appearance, such as page numbering, use of headers and footers, and use of footnotes.

Page Numbering:

If you need to number the pages of a document, but not the first page, use the **Insert, Page Numbers** command, which displays the following dialogue box:

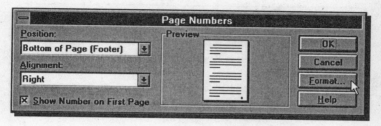

Use this box to specify the position of the page numbers in your document and their alignment. Selecting the **Format** button, opens another dialogue box, as shown below:

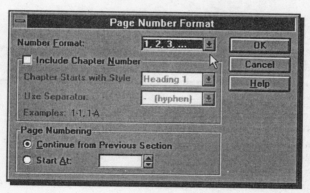

From this dialogue box you can select the **Number Format** from the following alternatives, '1, a, A, i, or I'; the more usual style being the first option, as used in this book. The 'Page Numbering' option gives you two alternatives; **Continue from Previous Section**, or **Start At** a specified number.

To illustrate page numbering open the PCUSERS7 document and use the **Insert, Page Numbers** command. Then, select 'Center' from the **Alignment** list box and make sure that the **Show Number on First Page** box is checked. Next, press the **Format** button, select **Start At 1** at the bottom of the second dialogue box, and press the **OK** button on each dialogue box. The result is a number '1' appearing centrally in a footer at the bottom of page 1, as shown below.

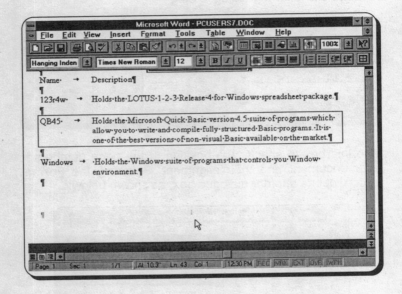

Using Headers and Footers:

Headers consist of text placed in the top margin area of a page, whereas footers are text in the bottom margin. Simple headers or footers in Word can consist of text and a page number, which are produced in the same position of every page in a document, while more complicated ones can also contain graphics images.

Word allows you to have one header/footer for the first page of a document, or section of a document, and a different one for the rest of the document. It also allows you to select a different header or footer for odd or even pages.

To insert a header or footer in a document, select the **View, Header and Footer** command, which causes Word to display the following:

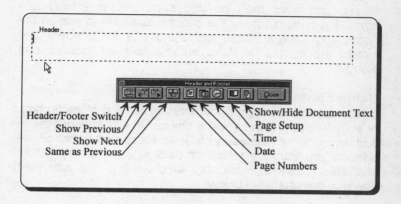

From here you can switch between header and footer by clicking the first button on the Header and Footer Bar. To adjust the horizontal position of a header or footer, use the 'Show Previous' and 'Show Next' buttons, or to adjust the vertical position of a header or footer use the 'Show Previous', 'Show Next' and 'Page Setup' buttons. These same three buttons can also be used to create a different header or footer for the first page of a document, or to create different headers and footers for odd and even pages.

In the example below, we chose to type 'Chapter 9' in the header panel, then we pressed <Tab> and typed 'Page' followed by a space, then pressed the 'Page Numbers' button on the Header and Footer Bar, which inserted the numeral 1, then we pressed <Tab> and pressed the time button.

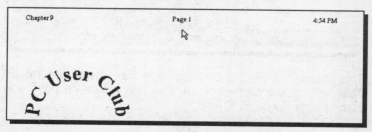

Once you select the **Close** button, headers and footers can be formatted and edited like any other text. To edit a header or footer, simply point to the appropriate panel and double-click. The Header and Footer Bar will appear on the screen and from then on you can use the editing and formatting commands, or the buttons available to you on the Formatting Toolbar. Note that the styles for headers and footers are named by Word automatically as 'Header' and 'Footer'.

Using Footnotes:

If your document requires footnotes at the end of each page, or endnotes at the end of each chapter, they are very easy to add and later, if necessary, to edit. Place the cursor at the position you want the reference point to be in the document and select **Insert, Footnote**, which opens the simulated dialogue boxes shown below:

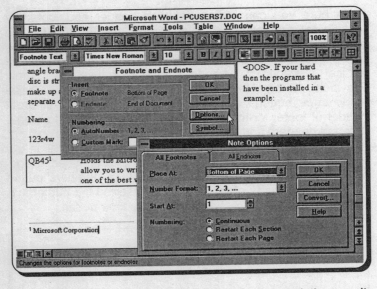

This displays both the two dialogue boxes and the results obtained, on the same screen. The first reference point was placed after the word 'QB45'.

118

The default option in the first dialogue box is **AutoNumber**. If you choose to press the **Options** button in this box, Word displays a second dialogue box from which you can select to place the footnote at the 'Bottom of the Page' or 'Beneath the Text'. You could also choose from this second dialogue box the number format, the starting number of the reference, and the numbering style.

If you wanted to type a reference mark of your own choosing, then select the **Custom Mark** from the first dialogue box. Pressing the **Symbol** button allows you the use of endless characters, particularly if you choose 'Wingdings' in the **Symbols from** list, as shown below.

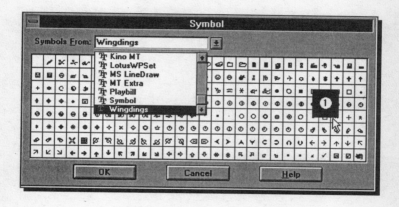

Once you have decided on your selection, save the resultant work under the filename PCUSERS8.

10. USING TABLES AND GRAPHS

The ability to use 'Tables' is built into most top-range word processors these days. At first glance the process might look complicated and perhaps only a small percentage of users take advantage of the facility, which is a pity because using a 'Table' has many possibilities. If you have worked with a spreadsheet, such as Excel or Lotus 1-2-3, then you are familiar with tables.

Tables are used to create adjacent columns of text and numeric data. A table is simply a grid of columns and rows with the intersection of a column and row forming a rectangular box which is referred to as a 'cell'. In Word you can include pictures, charts, notes, footnotes, tabs, and page breaks in your tables. There are several ways to place information into a table:

- Type the desired text, or numeric data.
- Paste text from the main document.
- Link two tables within a document.
- Insert data created in another application.
- Import a picture.
- Create a chart on information held in a table.

The data is placed into individual cells that are organised into columns and rows, similar to a spreadsheet. You can modify the appearance of table data by applying text formatting and enhancements, or by using different paragraph styles.

Creating a Table

Tables can be created either by pressing the 'Table' button on the toolbar, shown here, or by using the **Table, Insert Table** command. Using the latter, displays the dialogue box shown on the next page, which enables you to size the column widths at that point.

As an example we will step through the process of creating the table shown on the next page. Open the PCUSERS8 file, place the insertion point at the end of the file (or where you want the table), then click on the 'Table' button and drag down and to the right.

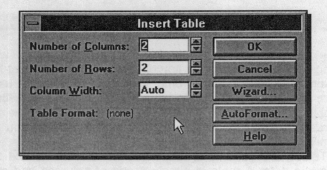

As you drag the mouse, the 'Table' button expands to create the grid of rows and columns. At the bottom of the box there is an automatic display of the number of rows and columns you are selecting by this method. When you release the mouse button, a table is inserted in your document the size of the selected grid.

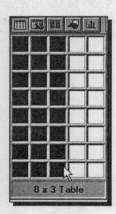

For our example, we require a 9 x 5 cell table. Once this appears in position, the cursor is placed in the top left cell awaiting your input. To see more clearly the cells forming the table, select the **Table, Gridlines** command to display the dotted lines around each cell.

To move around in a table, simply click the desired cell, or use one of the keyboard commands listed below.

Navigating with the Keyboard :

To navigate around a table when using the keyboard, use the following keys:

Press this	*To do this*
Tab	Moves the insertion point right one cell, in the same row, and from the last cell in one row to the first cell in the next row. If the cell contains information it highlights the contents.

Shift+Tab	Moves the insertion point left one cell. If the cell contains information it highlights the contents.
↑,↓,←, and →	Moves the insertion point within cells, between cells, and between the cells in a table and the main document text.
Home	Moves the insertion point to the beginning of the current line within a cell.
Alt+Home	Moves the insertion point to the first column in the current row.
End	Moves the insertion point to the end of the current line within a cell.
Alt+End	Moves the insertion point to the last column in the current row.
Alt+PgUp	Moves the insertion point to the top cell in the column.
Alt+PgDn	Moves the insertion point to the bottom cell in the column.

Now type in the information below and format your table using either the **Format, Paragraph** command or the buttons on the Formatting Toolbar to align the contents of the various columns as shown. The heading does not form part of the table. To change column width or row height, see next page.

Types of Removable Discs

Description	Capacity Kbytes	Price/Unit Pence	Number Bought	Cost in £
Double-sided floppies	360	40	20	
High-density floppies	1,200	60	40	
Double-sided stiffies	720	80	60	
High-density stiffies	1,440	100	80	
Removable hard discs	105,000	6500	1	
			Total	

Changing Column Width and Row Height:

The column width of selected cells or entire columns can be changed by dragging the table column markers on the ruler or by dragging the column boundaries, as shown in the adjacent display.

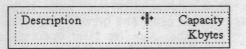

You can also drag a column boundary while holding down other keys. The overall effects of these actions is as follows:

Keys	Effect
No key	all columns to the right are re-sized proportionally with the overall width of the table remaining the same size.
Shift key	only the column to the right is re-sized with the overall width of the table remaining the same.
Ctrl key	all columns to the right become the same size which changes the overall width of the table.
Shift+Ctrl keys	all columns to the right retain their size which changes the overall width of the table.

The height of a row depends on its contents. As you type text into a cell, its height increases to accommodate it. You can also insert empty lines before or after the text by pressing the <Enter> key, which also increases the height of a cell. All other cells in that row become the same height as the largest cell.

The width of a column and the height of a row can also be changed by using the **Table, Cell Height and Width** command.

When you have finished, save your work under the filename PCUSERS9. We will use this table to show you how you can insert expressions into cells to make your table behave just like a spreadsheet.

124

Entering Expressions:

To enter an expression into a table's cell, so that you can carry out spreadsheet type calculations, highlight the cell and use the **Table, Formula** command which displays the following dialogue box:

Types of Removable Discs				
Description	Capacity Kbytes	Price/Unit Pence	Number Bought	Cost in £
Double-sided floppies	360	40	20	
High-density floppies	1,200	60	40	
Double-sided stiffies	720	80	60	
High-density stiffies	1,440	100	80	
Removable hard discs	105,000	6500	1	

Formula

Formula:
=SUM(LEFT)

OK
Cancel
Help

Number Format:

Paste Function: Paste Bookmark:

Word analyses the table and suggests an appropriate formula in the **Formula** box. In the above situation, it has found numbers in cells to the left of the highlighted cell, therefore it suggests the SUM(LEFT) formula. To replace this formula with another formula, simply delete it from the **Formula** box and type the new formula preceded by the equal (=) sign.

For example, to calculate the cost of purchased discs in Sterling (£) in cell E3, type the following formula in the **Formula** box:

```
=C3*D3/100
```

Word performs mathematical calculations on numbers in cells and inserts the result of the calculation as a field in the cell that contains the insertion pointer. Cells are referred to as A1, A2, B1, B2, and so on, with the letter representing a column and the number representing a row. Thus, B3 refers to the hatched cell.

125

When you use the **Table, Formula** command, Word assumes addition, unless you indicate otherwise, and proposes a sum based on the following rules:

- If the cell that contains the insertion pointer is at the intersection of a row and column and both contain numbers, Word sums the column. To sum the row, type =SUM(LEFT) or =SUM(RIGHT) in the **Formula** box, depending on the location of the insertion pointer.

- If the cell that contains the insertion pointer contains text or numbers, they are ignored.

- Word evaluates numbers beginning with the cell closest to the cell that contains the insertion pointer and continues until it reaches either a blank cell or a cell that contains text.

- If the numbers you are calculating include a number format, such as a £ sign, the result will also contain that format.

Fill in the rest of column E, then to calculate the total cost, place the insertion pointer in cell E9 and use the **Table, Formula** command. Word analyses your table and suggests the following function:

```
=SUM(ABOVE)
```

which is the correct formula in this case. On pressing **OK**, Word calculates the result and places it in cell E9. The completed table should look as follows:

Types of Removable Discs				
Description	Capacity Kbytes	Price/Unit Pence	Number Bought	Cost in £
Double-sided floppies	360	40	20	8
High-density floppies	1,200	60	40	24
Double-sided stiffies	720	80	60	48
High-density stiffies	1,440	100	80	80
Removable hard discs	105,000	6500	1	65
			Total	225

As the result of a calculation is inserted as a field in the cell that contains the insertion pointer, if you change the contents of the referenced cells, you must update the calculation. To do this, select the field (the cell that contains the formula) and press the **F9** function key.

In a formula you can specify any combination of mathematical and logical operators from the following list.

Addition	+
Subtraction	−
Multiplication	*
Division	/
Percent	%
Powers and roots	^
Equal to	=
Less than	<
Less than or equal to	<=
Greater than	>
Greater than or equal to	>=
Not equal to	< >

The following functions can accept references to table cells:

ABS( )	AND( )	AVERAGE( )
COUNT( )	DEFINED( )	FALSE( )
IF( )	INT( )	MAX( )
MIN( )	MOD( )	NOT( )
OR( )	PRODUCT( )	ROUND( )
SIGN( )	SUM( )	TRUE( )

The main reason for using formulae in a table, instead of just typing in the numbers, is that formulae will still give the correct final answer even if some of the data is changed. In this case you simply correct the data cells and Word recalculates the result once you update the field by pressing **F9**.

Editing a Table:

You can edit a table by inserting or deleting columns or rows, merging cells, or splitting a table.

To insert a row or column: Select where you want the new row or column to appear, remembering that the selected row (or column) and all rows below (or columns to its right) will move down (or to the right). Then you use the **Table, Insert Cells, Insert Entire Row** (or **Column**) command.

To delete a row or column: Select the row(s) or column(s) you want to delete, then use the **Table, Delete Cells, Delete Entire Row** (or **Column**) command.

To merge cells: Select the cells you want to merge, then use the **Table, Merge Cells** command. This command can be used to merge several cells to provide room for a table heading.

To split a table: Move the insertion pointer to where you want to split the table, then use the **Table, Split Cells** command. A blank line appears above the current row in the table, splitting it into two separate tables.

Formatting a Table:

You can enhance the looks of a table by selecting one of several pre-defined styles. To do this, place the insertion pointer in a cell of your table and use the **Table, Table AutoFormat** command. Select Classic 2 from the **Formats** list, to produce the display below and save it as TABLE1.

Description	Capacity Kbytes	Price/Unit Pence	Number Bought	Cost in £
Double-sided floppies	360	40	20	8
High-density floppies	1,200	60	40	24
Double-sided stiffies	720	80	60	48
High-density stiffies	1,440	100	80	80
Removable hard discs	105,000	6500	1	65
			Total	225

Using Microsoft Graph

To chart your Word data, you can use Microsoft Graph, which is a separate program from Word. However, the program is designed to work with Word because it supports OLE (Object Linking and Embedding).

You can activate Graph by pressing the Graph button on the Standard Toolbar, shown here. Alternatively, you can use the **Insert, Object** command and select 'Microsoft Graph' from the list in the Object dialogue box, shown below:

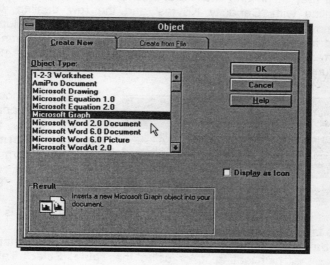

Microsoft Graph opens in an application window on top of Word, with default data in its data sheet. To change this default chart, you must change the data in the default data sheet. This can be done in various ways, but the easiest way is to either type your data directly into the displayed data sheet, or select the data from a Word table before activating Graph.

To demonstrate the way in which you can chart data held in a Word table, open the TABLE1 and then use your editing skills to first remove the AutoFormatting, then transform the table to what is displayed overleaf.

Removable Discs	Price p/Unit	No. Bought	Cost in £
Double-sided floppies	40	20	8.00
High-density floppies	60	40	24.00
Double-sided stiffies	80	60	48.00
High-density stiffies	100	80	80.00

Note that we have replaced 'Description' with 'Removable Discs', and that we have abbreviated the column headings so that they fit on one line. Also, we have deleted the column dealing with 'Capacity KBytes' and the row dealing with removable hard discs. However, having deleted a column, and in order to change the format of the 'Costs' column to currency, you must retype the formulae in what is now column D.

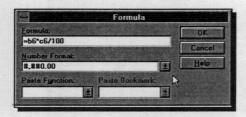

To do this choose the appropriate format from the **Number Format** list of the Formula dialogue box, as shown here. The entry in the **Formula** box is for the last row of the Costs column of our table.

Save the resultant work as TABLE2. Then select the table, by either highlighting it, or using the **Table, Select Table** command, and activate Microsoft Graph. If you don't select a table, Graph displays its default table and chart, as follows:

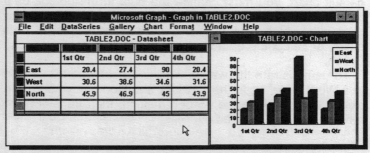

If you select the table, what should appear on your screen, after Graph displays its default table and associated chart, is:

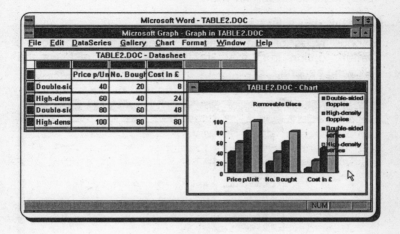

Note that the text we included in cell A1, was taken by Graph as the title for our chart.

You can add various items to a chart, such as titles, data labels, floating text, legends, arrows and gridlines. All these can be added with the use of the **Chart** command which displays an appropriate sub-menu with all the required options, as shown below.

When you close the Graph application, you can embed the chart in your Word document; you will be asked whether you want to update the document. If you answer with **Yes**, then Word will include your chart within a frame and place it under the table containing the data from which it was drawn.

To access Microsoft Graph double-click at the frame containing your chart. Graph will be activated with the chart ready in place for further work.

Types of Charts:

Various types of charts can be selected by choosing the **Gallery** option from the Graph menu, which displays the following options:

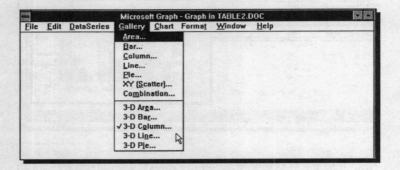

Selecting any one of these **Gallery** options, displays a choice of up to 8 separate types of charts. For example, selecting the **3-D Area** option, displays the following:

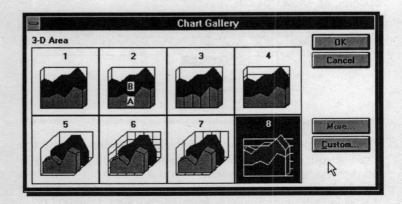

To see your chart in a different form, select your chart, then choose one of the displayed options and press **OK**. Your graph is immediately redrawn to reflect your choice of chart type. Try some of these options and watch the results.

The chart types available in the **Gallery** sub-menu (described from top to bottom), are normally used to show the following relationships between data:

Area	for comparing value changes to the total over a period of time. The 100% option shows relationships to the whole.
Bar	for comparing differences in data. Displays the values of dependent variables as two-dimensional horizontal bars. The stacked and 100% options show relationships to the whole.
Column	for comparing differences in data over a period of time. Displays the values of dependent variables as two-dimensional vertical columns. The stacked and 100% options show relationships to the whole.
Line	for representing data values with points joined by lines and appearing at equal intervals along the x-axis. For such charts, the x-axis could be intervals in time, such as labels representing months.
Pie	for comparing parts with the whole. Displays data blocks as slices of a pie. Can contain only one series.
XY (Scatter)	for showing the relationship, or degree of relationship, between numeric values in different groups of data. Used for finding patterns or trends in data (whether variables are dependent on or affect one another).

Combination	for displaying related data measured in different units (up to four axes can be used in a combination chart); used for comparing two different kinds of data or to show a correlation that might be difficult to recognise.

Improving a Word Chart:

A Word chart is in fact a Microsoft Draw file. Each value in the data used to create the chart, is a separate object within the chart. You can edit the chart by selecting either the **Chart** or **Format** command. You can then use any of the sub-menu options to move or modify selected objects, including text objects, or create new objects in the chart.

In the example shown below, the title of the chart was edited by selecting it and then using the **Format**, **Font** command and choosing size 12; the legend object was moved to the bottom of the chart by selecting it and using the **Format**, **Legend** command then choosing the Bottom option, and the height of the chart was increased to accommodate the new legend position without diminishing the actual size of the chart columns. Finally, an arrow was added, to emphasise a point, by using the **Chart, Add Arrow** command, then moving it appropriately. Try all these options.

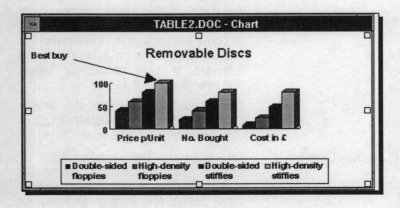

Adding Floating Text:

To add the floating text against the arrow, shown above, make sure that no other text is selected, and then just type what you want to appear on your chart. Your text appears in a box surrounded by black handles, indicating that it can be re-sized and moved. When you finish moving the text to its required position, press <Esc>, or click outside it.

When you have carried out all these changes to your chart within Graph, return to your document using the **File, Update** command, then save the changed Word document as TABLE3, using the **File, Save As** command.

We are sure that you will get many hours of fun with the various features of Microsoft Graph and, more to the point, produce some very professional graphics for your report presentations within Word.

11. MANAGING LARGE DOCUMENTS

Many users' needs might demand that they work with either large documents, or with documents which are split into many files; they might even have to automate certain routines. In such cases, knowing something about outlines, file management and design of macros is imperative.

Outline Mode

Outline mode provides a way of viewing and organising the contents of a document. Nine outline levels can be used and these could be based on formatted headings (Heading 1, Heading 2, through to Heading 8), plus Normal text. By assigning each heading level a different paragraph style, it allows easy assimilation of the contents of a document.

The following display shows part of the first page of Chapter 1 of this book in the Normal editing view.

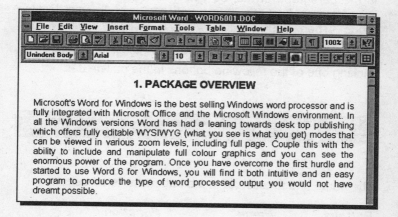

The same chapter is shown on the next page in outline view by either pressing the Outline button on the scroll bar, or selecting the **View, Outline** command. However, before you can see exactly what is shown here, you must assign styles to the various Headings. This can be done by selecting the outline view and assigning heading levels to your work using the tools on the outline bar which replaces the ruler.

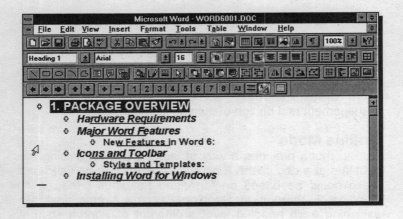

Assigning Outline Levels:

'Outline' levels are stored as part of the formatting information in the paragraph styles, so you must assign these levels to your paragraph styles before you can usefully use 'Outline' mode. Then your outline will automatically display your document headings at the correct levels. This is an easy process carried out by selecting an existing heading and clicking one of the following buttons in the outline bar:

The name and function of these buttons is listed below.

Buttons	Name	Function
←	**Promote**	Assigns heading to a higher outline level.
→	**Demote**	Assigns to a lower outline level.
⇒	**Double Arrow**	Demotes a heading to body text.

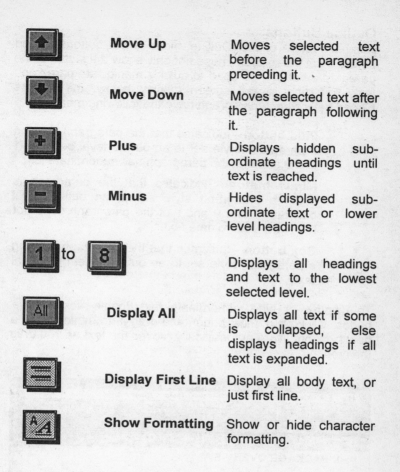

Move Up — Moves selected text before the paragraph preceding it.

Move Down — Moves selected text after the paragraph following it.

Plus — Displays hidden subordinate headings until text is reached.

Minus — Hides displayed subordinate text or lower level headings.

1 to 8 — Displays all headings and text to the lowest selected level.

Display All — Displays all text if some is collapsed, else displays headings if all text is expanded.

Display First Line — Display all body text, or just first line.

Show Formatting — Show or hide character formatting.

Using the expand and collapse commands, you can display the entire document or only selected text. Editing a document in 'Outline' mode is simple because you can control the level of detail that displays and quickly see the structure of the document. If you want to focus on the main topics in the document, you can collapse the text to display only paragraph styles set to high outline levels. If you want to view additional detail, you can expand the text to display text using paragraph styles set to lower outline levels.

Outline Buttons:

Another feature of the 'Outline' mode is the buttons placed before each paragraph. These not only show the status of the paragraph, but can be used to quickly manipulate paragraph text. Referring to the screen display below, the buttons placed before each paragraph have the following meaning:

     ⊕   **Plus button** - Indicates that the paragraph is using a paragraph style set to an outline level between 1 and 9 and that the paragraph has subordinate text.

     ▭   **Minus button** - Indicates that the paragraph is using a paragraph style set to an outline level between 1 and 9 and that the paragraph does not have any subordinate text.

     ▫   **Box button** - Indicates that the paragraph is using a paragraph style set to an outline level of Normal text.

To display, or hide, subordinate text double-click a 'Plus' button. Click on a 'Plus' button and drag it, to move text to a new location. Word automatically moves the text as you drag the mouse.

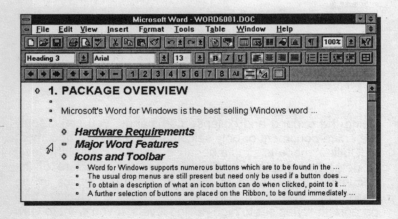

If you print from 'Outline' mode only the text that is exposed on the screen will actually print. Outline buttons do not print.

Outline Numbering:

If you want all your paragraphs numbered, you must rank all the styles and then assign one of the numbering schemes in the dialogue box obtained with the use of the **Format, Bullets and Numbering** command, and click the **Multilevel** tab to obtain the dialogue box shown below.

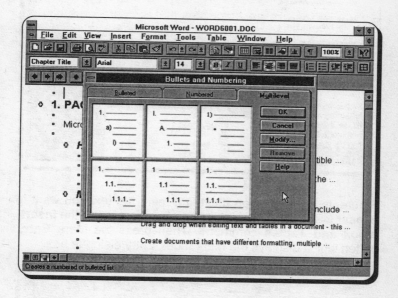

You could, of course, select the **Bulleted** or **Numbered** tabs, if you prefer.

Creating Table of Contents or an Index:

To create a table of contents, position the insertion point where you want the table of contents to appear, and use the **Insert, Index and Tables** command, then click the **Table of Contents** tab of the displayed dialogue box.

On pressing **OK** the table of contents is formed, as shown in the composite screen dump overleaf, ready for you to format to your requirements.

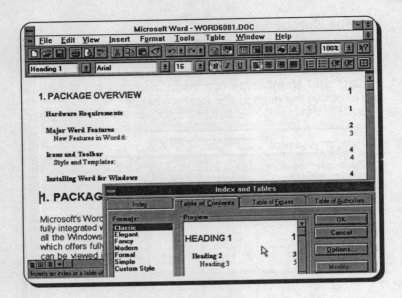

To create an index, you must first mark the text you want to appear in the index by highlighting it, before using the **Insert, Index and Tables** command. Then press the **Mark Entry** button which displays the Mark Index Entry dialogue box.

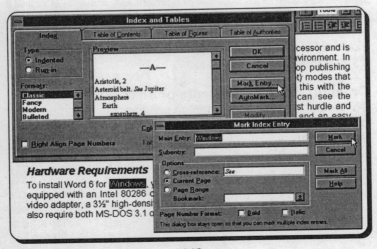

File Management

The first time you use the **File**, **Find File** command, Word searches the current directory and produces a list of available files and displays them within the following dialogue box.

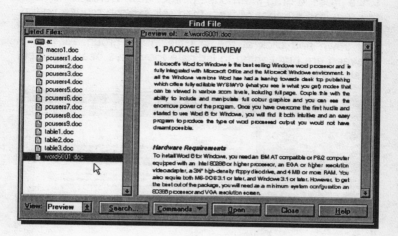

The first file is normally highlighted and its contents are displayed in the **Preview of** box. As you select another file from the list, Word displays its contents too.

You can change what is shown in the above listing by pressing the **Commands** button and selecting **Sorting** from

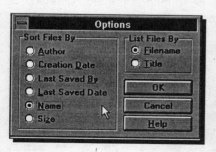

the list of commands, which displays the dialogue box shown here. From this box, you can select one of the 'Sort Files By' options, to have files listed by author, date, name of last person who saved the files, date with most recent date first, name of file (the default option), or size of file. File names can be listed by filename or by title, such as Package Overview or Memo to PC Users.

Once you have selected the options for the display of your files, you can select a file from the list by clicking on its name. A double-click opens the file. To select a group of files, point to the first file in the group, press the left mouse button and while pressed drag the mouse pointer downwards to highlight the required number of files, then release the mouse button. Alternatively, click at the first file in the group, hold the <Shift> key down and click at the last file in the group. All files in between are highlighted to indicate they have been selected, as shown below:

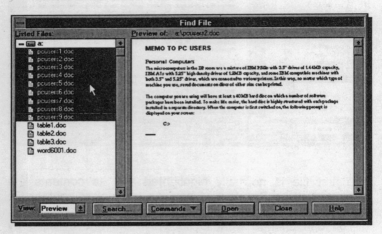

Once selected, files can be opened, printed, deleted, or copied, using the **Commands** button.

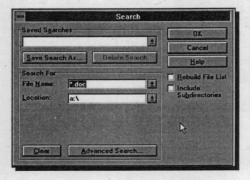

If you want to search for a different type of file, and/or for files in a different directory, then click the **Search** button to display the dialogue box shown here, and specify **Location**.

Assembling a Master Document

If you are involved in writing long documents, such as books, it is best if you split each document into sections (or chapters) of approximately 20 pages long. Anything above this length, particularly if it contains graphics, will strain your computer's resources. How much strain is experienced depends on how fast your computer is and how much Random Access Memory (RAM) it contains. In any case, large files take longer to open and save.

Having broken a long document into smaller sections you can work with these separately until you need to print your work in its entirety, or create a table of contents and an index with the page numbers. You will then need to create a 'Master Document'.

One method of doing this is to open a new document in Word, then use the **View, Master Document** command which will display the Master Document toolbar. Next, press the 'Insert Subdocument' button on the toolbar and select the file you want to insert into your Master Document (last file first), as shown below.

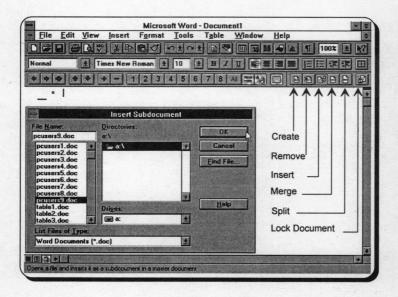

Printing a Master Document:

When you are finally ready to print the Master Document to paper, you can do so in two ways. To print the entire Master Document, print it from Normal view. To print only the outline of the Master Document, print it from Master Document view.

You could, of course, control the amount of detail you print by expanding or collapsing headings to display as much of the document as you require.

12. WORD MACROS

Word Macro Basics

A macro is simply a set of instructions made up of a sequence of keystrokes, mouse selections, or commands stored in a macro file. After saving, or writing, a macro and attaching a quick key combination to it, you can run the same sequence of commands whenever you want. This can save a lot of time and, especially with repetitive operations, can save mistakes creeping into your work.

In Word there are two basic ways of creating macros. The first one is generated by the program itself, recording and saving a series of keystrokes, or mouse clicks. The second one involves the use of WordBasic, the programming language that comes with Word for Windows. With this method, you can write quite complex macro programs directly into a macro file using the Word for Windows' macro editor.

Where to Store Macros:

You can choose where to store macros, whether you record them or program them, with the **File, Templates** command which displays the following dialogue box:

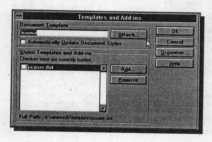

By default, Word stores macros in the **Normal.dot** template, making them accessible to all documents. However, it is sensible to save specialised macros with your document template rather than clutter the **Normal.dot** file with too many macros.

If you assign macros to a named template other than the default, you can use the Organizer to manage them. For example, use the **Attach** button and select the **macro.dot** template that contains macros that come with Word, as shown at the top of the next page. Pressing **OK** and clicking the **Organizer** button on the Templates and Add-ins dialogue box, displays the Organizer dialogue box.

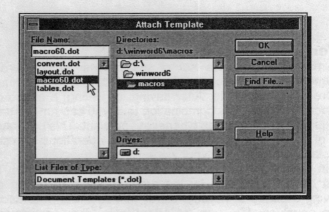

Finally, pressing the Macros tab, produces the dialogue box:

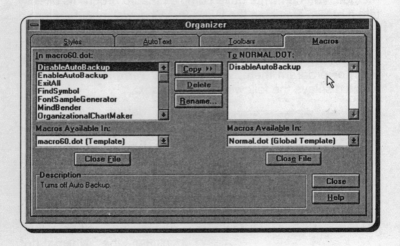

From here, you can manage your macros by copying them into different templates, deleting them or renaming them.

Macros can also be stored in a third way, as 'Commands', but when you record, or program them, they can only be stored as global or with a document template. Macros stored as 'Commands' are built-in macros stored within Word, many of which appear as menu commands. These and others, that do not appear as menu commands, can be added to a toolbar button or your own macro.

To see what macro 'Commands' are available, use the **Tools, Macro** command, and select Word Commands from the **Macros Available In** list box, shown here.

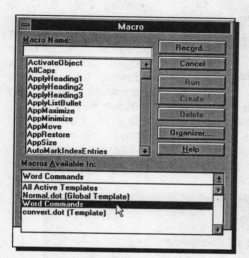

There are over 300 macro 'Commands' and as each one is selected, by high-lighting it, an explanation of what it does appears in the **Description** box at the bottom of the dialogue box. It is perhaps worth spending some time examining what is available, particularly if you intend to write your own macros.

Recording a Macro:

To demonstrate how easy it is to save and name a macro, we will start with a simplistic one that enhances the word at the cursor to bold type in italics. Open PCUSERS1.DOC, place the cursor in a document word and either double-click the **REC** button on the Status bar, shown below, or select the

Tools, Macro command and press the **Record** button on the displayed Macro dialogue box. Either of these, opens the Record Macro dialogue box shown on the next page.

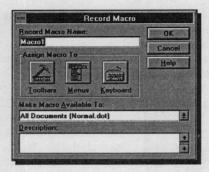

Type a name for your macro (call it Bolditlc) in the **Record Macro Name** input box, then give your macro a **Description** (such as Bold & Italic) and click on the **Keyboard** button. In the displayed Customize dialogue box, press a suitable key stroke combination, such as <Ctrl+Shift+I>, in the **Press New Shortcut Key** input box. The shortcut key combination will appear in the input box and immediately below it you will be informed whether this key combination is currently attached to an internal macro or not, as shown below:

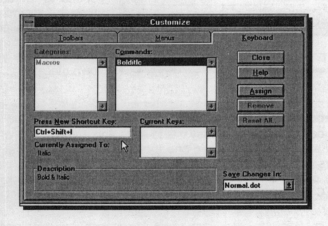

Most <Ctrl> or <Shift> keys with a letter or function key combinations are suitable (the word [unassigned] will appear under the **Currently Assigned To:** heading) if the chosen combination of keys is not already assigned to a macro. Our choice of key stokes results in the message 'Italic', under the **Currently Assigned To:** heading. This does not matter in this instance, because both the key combinations <Ctrl+I> and <Ctrl+Shift+I> are assigned to Italic, so we can use one.

Finally, press the **Assign** button followed by the **Close** button.

 From this point on, all key strokes and mouse clicks (but not mouse movements in the editing area) will be recorded. To indicate that the recorder is on, Word attaches a recorder graphic to the mouse pointer, as shown here.

Word also displays the Stop and Pause buttons on the Macro Record toolbar to allow you to stop or pause a macro. A macro can also be stopped by double-clicking at the REC button on the Status bar.

While the cursor is still placed in the word to be modified, use the key strokes, <Ctrl+→> to move to the end of the current word, followed by <Shift+Ctrl+←>, to highlight the word, click the Bold and Italic buttons on the Formatting toolbar, press <→> to cancel the highlight and click the Stop button on the Macro Record toolbar. Your macro should now be recorded and held in memory.

Saving a Macro to Disc:

To save your macro to disc, use the **File, Save All** command and give your macro the name MACRO1. If you quit Word without saving the template, you will be asked if you want to save the changes made to the template. Choose the **Yes** button to save your macro.

Playing Back a Macro:

There are four main ways of running a macro. You can use the playback shortcut keys straight from the keyboard; in our case place the cursor in another word and press <Ctrl+Shift+I>. The word should be enhanced automatically. If not, check back that you carried out the instructions correctly.

The second method is to select the **Tools, Macro** command, then select the macro from the list, as shown on the next page, and press the **Run** button. From this dialogue box you can also **Edit, Delete,** or select the **Organizer** so that you can **Rename** macros.

The last two methods of activating a macro are to attach it to a custom button on a toolbar or a menu, and simply click the button or the menu option.

Attaching Macros to a Toolbar or a Menu:

To assign a macro to a toolbar or a menu, use the **Tools, Customize** command, and select **Macros** from the **Categories** list of the displayed dialogue box, shown on the top half of the next page. Next, click the macro from the **Macros** list to see its description and drag the macro name to any button on the toolbars. The selected macro replaces the original function of the button.

To assign a macro to a menu, click the **Menus** tab of the Customize dialogue box, select **Macros** from the **Categories** list on the displayed dialogue box, shown on the bottom half of the next page, and press the **Add** button. Next, click the **Menu Bar** button, type an entry in the **Name on Menu Bar** input box. Finally, select the **Position on Menu Bar** on which the entry should appear.

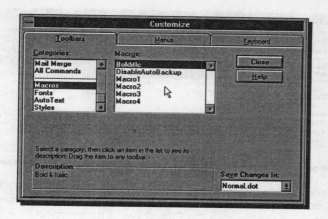

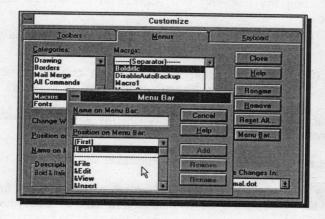

Editing a Macro:

You can edit the entries in a macro file by selecting the **Tools**, **Macros**, command which opens the Macro dialogue box in which you select the macro file to edit. Select the 'Bolditlc' file, assuming of course that you saved it with that name, and press the **Edit** button. Word loads the file into the normal editing screen and you treat the macro file exactly the same as any other. The listing of our Bolditlc file should look as follows:

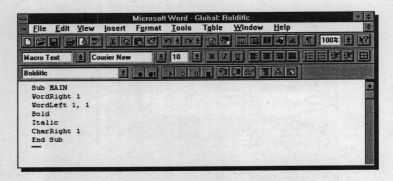

```
Sub MAIN
WordRight 1
WordLeft 1, 1
Bold
Italic
CharRight 1
End Sub
```

If you look at this listing you will see that it would be very easy to edit the commands in the file. If you do edit it, you should then save the file with the **File, Save All** command.

Notice the following two aspects in the screen display above:

(a) When editing a macro, the Ruler is replaced by a Macro Editing bar, and

(b) Macros within WordBasic are considered to be 'subroutines' that run under Word for Windows.

The buttons on the Macro Editing bar have the following functions:

Button	*Name*	*Function*
	Record	Displays the Record Macro dialogue box so that you can begin to record a macro.
	Record Next C'nd	Records the next command you choose and inserts the corresponding WordBasic instruction in the active macro-editing window.
	Start	Runs the active macro which must be opened in a macro-editing window.

154

	Trace	Runs the macro from start to finish, one statement at a time, highlighting the statement being executed.
	Continue	Continues to run a paused macro.
	Stop	Stops recording or running a macro.
	Step	Runs a macro one statement at a time, highlighting the statement and pausing until the Step button is pressed again.
	Step Subs	Executes the macro one subroutine at a time, highlighting the first line of the following subroutine and pausing until the Step Subs button is pressed again.
	Show Variables	Shows the current value of the variables used in the macro and allows you to reset these during macro execution.
	Add/Remove REM	Adds REM statements to or removes them from the selected lines in a macro-editing window. REM statements are ignored during macro execution.
	Macro	Records a macro, runs any macro or standard Word command, or opens a macro for editing.
	Dialog Editor	Starts the Dialog Editor, if it is not already running, and switches to it.

It is easy to make small changes to macros you have recorded using the buttons on the Macro Editing bar. However, if you wanted to create a macro that executed commands which could not be recorded, such as switching to a particular directory and displaying the Open dialogue box, then you must learn to use Word's macro language, WordBasic.

To learn to program in WordBasic, you can order the Microsoft Word Developer's Kit with the coupon included in your Word package.

Alternatively, if you have installed the complete Word package, then WordBasic Help should have been installed. If that is the case, then you could view the online reference on WordBasic by choosing Contents from the Help menu and clicking the WordBasic Help entry. There is a wealth of information in WordBasic Help which will show you how to program your macros and how to use the various built-in functions. Try it, you will learn a lot.

APPENDIX A
KEYBOARD SHORTCUTS

Shortcuts for Activating Commands:

To execute commands quickly, press the following key combinations:

Command	Press
To start a New document	Ctrl +N
To Open a document	Ctrl+O
To Save a document	Ctrl+S
To Print a document	Ctrl+P
To Undo an edit or command	Ctrl+Z
To Repeat Undo	Ctrl+Y
To Cut a selected block	Ctrl+X
To Copy a selected block	Ctrl+C
To Paste a cut or copied block	Ctrl+V
To Clear a selected block	Del
To Select All (entire document)	Ctrl+A
To Find specified text or formatting	Ctrl+F
To Find and Replace text or formatting	Ctrl+H
To Go To a specified page	Ctrl+G
To activate the Spelling tool	F7
To activate the Thesaurus tool	Shift+F7
To select a Table (5 on the numeric keyboard)	Alt+5

Shortcuts for Navigating and SelectingText:

You can move the cursor around a document with the normal direction keys, and with the key combinations shown below. To select text, press the <Shift> key and hold it pressed prior to using the navigational key combinations:

To Move	Press
Left one character	←
Right one character	→
Up one line	↑
Down one line	↓
Left one word	Ctrl+←
Right one word	Ctrl+→

To beginning of line	Home
To end of line	End
To paragraph beginning	Ctrl+↑
To paragraph end	Ctrl+↓
Up one screen	PgUp
Down one screen	PgDn
To top of previous page	Ctrl+PgUp
To top of next page	Ctrl+PgDn
To beginning of file	Ctrl+Home
To end of file	Ctrl+End

In a multi-page document, use <Ctrl+G> to jump to a specified page number.

Advanced Search Operators:

The list below gives the key combinations of special characters to type into the **Find What** and **Replace With** boxes when the **Use Pattern Matching** box is checked.

To find or replace	*Type*
Any single character. For example, searching for nec?, will find such words as necessary, neck, nectar, connect, etc.	?
Any string of characters. For example, searching for c*r, will find such words as cellar, character, chillier, etc.	*
One of the specified characters. For example, searching for d[oi]g, will find such words as dog and dig.	[ ]
Any single character in specified range. For example, searching for [b-f]ore, will find such words as bore, core, fore, etc.	[-]
Any single character except the one inside the brackets. For example, searching for l[!o]ve, will find live, but not love.	[!]

Any single character except characters in the range inside the brackets. For example, searching for [!s-z]ong, will find long but not song.	[!s-z]
Exactly n occurrences of the previous character. For example, searching for me{2}t, will find meet but not met.	{n}
At least n occurrences of the previous character. For example, searching for me{1,}t, will find met and meet.	{n,}
From n to m occurrences of the previous character. For example, searching for 9{1,3}, will find 9, 99, and 999.	{n,m}
One or more occurrences of the previous character. For example, searching for ro@t, will find rot and root.	@
The beginning of a word. For example, searching for <on, will find on and onto, but not upon.	<
The end of a word. For example, searching for >on, will find on and upon, but not onto.	>

Text Formatting with Quick Keys:

To format selected text, use the following shortcut keys.

To Format	*Type*
Bold	Ctrl+B
Italic	Ctrl+I
Underline	Ctrl+U
Word underline	Ctrl+Shift+W
Double underline	Ctrl+Shift+D
Subscript	Ctrl+=
Superscript	Ctrl+Shift+=
Small caps	Ctrl+Shift+K

All caps	Ctrl+Shift+A
Change case letters	Shift+F3
Hide text	Ctrl+Shift+H
Copy formats	Ctrl+Shift+C
Paste formats	Ctrl+Shift+V
Remove formats	Ctrl+Space
Next larger font size	Ctrl+>
Next smaller font size	Ctrl+<

Paragraph Alignment Shortcuts:

You can align a paragraph at the left margin (the default), at the right margin, centred between both margins, or justified between both margins. This can be achieved as follows:

To Format	*Type*
Left align	Ctrl+L
Centre align	Ctrl+E
Right align	Ctrl+R
Justify	Ctrl+J
Indent from left margin	Ctrl+M
Decrease indent	Ctrl+Shift+M
Create a hanging indent	Ctrl+T
Decrease a hanging indent	Ctrl+Shift+T
Add or remove 12 points of space before a paragraph	Ctrl+0 (zero)
Remove paragraph formats not applied by a style	Ctrl+Q
Restore default formatting by applying the Normal style	Ctrl+Shift+N
Display or hide non-printing characters (such as · → ¶)	Ctrl+*

Paragraph Spacing Shortcuts:

To display a paragraph on screen or printed on paper in single-line, 1½-line, or double-line spacing, use the following:

To Format	*Type*
Single-spaced lines	Ctrl+1
One-and-a-half-spaced lines	Ctrl+5
Double-spaced lines	Ctrl+2

APPENDIX B
WORD'S TOOLBAR BUTTONS

The Standard Toolbar Buttons:

The Standard Toolbar contains 22 buttons which have the following effect:

Button	*Effect*
	Creates a new document based on the NORMAL.DOT template.
	Opens an existing document or template.
	Saves the active document or template.
	Prints the active document using the current defaults.
	Prints a preview of the document on screen.
	Checks the spelling in the active document.
	Cuts the selection and puts it on the clipboard.
	Copies the selection and puts it on the clipboard.
	Pastes the clipboard contents at the insertion point.

Paints the format of a selection at the insertion point.

 Undoes the last action.

 Redoes the last action.

 AutoFormats selection.

 Inserts AutoText.

 Inserts a table.

 Insert a Microsoft Excel worksheet.

 Changes the column format within selected sections.

 Starts Microsoft Draw.

 Starts Microsoft Graph.

 Displays or hides special non-printing characters, such as tabs or hard returns.

 Scales the document to 100% in the normal view.

 Provides help on an item by pointing to it.

162

The Formatting Toolbar Buttons:

The Formatting Toolbar contains 12 buttons which have the following effect:

Button	Effect
B	Embolden or clear selected text.
I	Italicise or clear selected text.
U	Underline or clear selected text.
	Left-align selected paragraphs.
	Centre-align selected paragraphs.
	Right-align selected paragraphs.
	Justify selected paragraphs.
	Creates a numbered list based on the current defaults.
	Creates a bulleted list based on the current defaults.
	Moves the left indent to the previous tab stop.
	Moves the left indent to the next tab stop.
	Inserts a border.

INDEX

NOTES

COMPANION DISC TO THIS BOOK

This book contains many pages of file/program listings. There is no reason why you should spend hours typing them into your computer, unless you wish to do so, or need the practice.

The COMPANION DISC for this book comes with all the example listings. It is available in both 3.5-inch and 5.25-inch formats.

COMPANION DISCS for all books written by the same author(s) and published by BERNARD BABANI (publishing) LTD, are also available and are listed at the front of this book. Make sure you fill in your name and address and specify the book number, title and the disc size in your order.

ORDERING INSTRUCTIONS

To obtain your copy of the companion disc, fill-in the order form below, enclose a cheque (payable to **P.R.M. Oliver**) or a postal order, and send it to the address given below.

Book No.	Book Name	Unit Price	Total Price
BP		£3.50	
BP		£3.50	
BP		£3.50	
Name .... Address		Sub-total	£.............
		P & P (@ 45p/disc)	£.............
Disc Format 3.5-inch....... 5.25-inch......		Total Due	£.............
Send to: P.R.M. Oliver, CSM, Pool, Redruth, Cornwall, TR15 3SE			